Sailing By

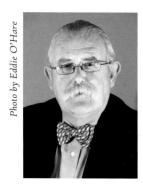

Photo by Eddie O'Hare

About the Editor

Marcus Connaughton presents and produces RTÉ Radio 1's maritime programme, *Seascapes*. A veteran of the Irish record industry, he joined RTÉ as a radio producer in the late 1980s. Over the past twenty-five years, he has produced a wide range of programming from the *Metal Show* on 2FM to *Bluestime* on RTÉ Radio 1. He is the author of *Rory Gallagher: His Life and Times*.

Sailing By

Celebrating 25 Years of
Seascapes on RTÉ Radio 1

Edited by
Marcus Connaughton

The Liffey Press

Published by
The Liffey Press Ltd
Raheny Shopping Centre, Second Floor
Raheny, Dublin 5, Ireland
www.theliffeypress.com

A catalogue record of this book is
available from the British Library.

ISBN 978-1-908308-66-5

Printed in Spain by GraphyCems

Contents

Foreword

Mark Mellett

For most people it would be a privilege to be asked to write the foreword for a book, but when the book is an edited compendium by Marcus Connaughton celebrating the 25th anniversary of *Seascapes*, the privilege is an honour. No radio program has done more to institutionalise a maritime constituency in Ireland than *Seascapes*.

Ireland needs a strong maritime constituency. Few citizens appreciate that Ireland lays claim to a jurisdiction which is almost three times the size of Germany, 92 per cent of which is under water. An area where the sovereignty and sovereign rights translate into the property rights of our citizens. Our land/sea interface offers one of the most spectacular and beautiful coastlines in the world. In terms of wealth, our seas are rich in biodiversity with vulnerable marine ecosystems that are critical to food production. Some estimates suggest that our seas hold potentially trillions of euros in yet to be found mineral and hydrocarbon resources. The potential from harnessing maritime wind and wave energy is extraordinary. With almost 99 per cent of our trade by volume carried by sea, our sea lines of communications and ports are the lifelines of our economy.

Ireland's rich maritime heritage defines us as a people and society. Almost 500 years ago the ships of the Warrior Queen Grace O'Malley ruled our west coast. One thousand years earlier St Brendan explored the Atlantic ocean and its hostile seas, discovering new territories. Together these eras reflect the birthright of our maritime nation. An island of saints and scholars, an island of explorers and warriors who valued, understood and protected the sea. Names like John Holland, Louis Brennan, Admiral William Brown and Commodore John Barry are just a few of our maritime heroes known across the oceans. The first nominee for the Victoria Cross was Rear Admiral Charles Davis Lucas from Armagh.

As a society it is our duty to uphold our sovereignty and sovereign rights while also meeting our legal obligations. Sovereign rights that are not upheld are more imaginary than real. It is for this reason that every hour of every day our Defence Forces underwrite our sovereignty with the men and women of the Naval Service patrolling what are statistically some of the most hostile seas in the world. Today we are at the dawn of a new era for maritime Ireland. An era stimulated by the growing realisation of maritime-linked economic opportunities. Our economy will be enhanced by appropriate governance of our maritime domain. Governance will be built on norms and principles such as sustainable development and adaptation. It will facilitate an industry-led approach to research and development through an ecosystem of innovation that will yield intellectual property, high potential start-up companies and jobs in the smart economy. Higher education institutes and national bodies such as the Defence Forces, the Marine Institute and clusters such as the Irish Maritime and Energy Resource Cluster will inform good governance supporting enterprise, improving services and enhancing security. Good governance will be reinforced by consultation with and engagement by civil society nurturing a strong maritime constituency.

Creating a maritime constituency requires champions and that is exactly what the contributors to this reflection are. Creating a maritime constituency also requires competent maritime thought leaders like Marcus Connaughton, Tom MacSweeney and Lorna Siggins. In the final analysis it is political will and leadership together with a discerning constituency, shaping governance with civil society, government and market actors that will secure our birthright as a maritime nation with its 'power by land and sea'.

Rear Admiral Mark Mellett DSM
Deputy Chief of Staff
Defence Forces Ireland/Óglaigh na hÉireann

Preface

Tom McGuire

It is great to have an opportunity to mark a special milestone in the history of Irish radio on the twenty-fifth anniversary of the first edition of *Seascapes* on RTÉ Radio 1. It is a particular tribute to the foresight, dedication and professionalism of RTÉ's former Marine Correspondent, Tom MacSweeney, whose brainchild the first programme was, that has earned such an enduring place in the RTÉ Radio 1 schedule.

The first strains of 'Sailing By' on an evening are 'a call to hear' and perhaps the greatest tribute that can be paid to *Seascapes* is the many listeners who profess to have no connection with marine life or leisure and yet make an appointment to listen.

In a special way *Seascapes* opens the hatch on the maritime community and welcomes the rest of the world on board. Over the last quarter of a century presenters, reporters and contributors to the programme have brought us to far-flung exotic places and back home to the isles, inlets and waterways of Ireland.

For the maritime and fishing industry *Seascapes* has often become a forum that saw issues and opinions critical to development and survival at its centre.

In the archive of a quarter of a century of broadcasting, *Seascapes* has created an invaluable national resource which reflects the

the characters, events and developments in the Irish and international maritime world.

The development of technology has made the programme more accessible to contributors and the audience over the years, and many memorable outside broadcasts have forged important links for *Seascapes* and RTÉ in local and regional communities. The dedication of all staff, whether in studio, on location or either side of the microphone, has been a critical ingredient of the success of *Seascapes*.

For two decades Tom MacSweeney was at the helm of the good ship. In the past five years Marcus Connaughton has assumed a producer/presenter role and his dedication and professionalism have ensured that *Seascapes* has continued as one of the few year-round features programmes in the RTÉ Radio 1 schedule.

It is good that this publication can mark the silver jubilee of a programme bookended by Tom and Marcus, and may I wish *Seascapes* 'fair sailing' as it embarks on the next leg of the voyage.

Tom McGuire
Head of RTÉ Radio 1

Acknowledgements

Marcus Connaughton

Many thanks to the many contributors and organisations who have supported this project.

Instantly recognisable from its opening bars, 'Sailing By' was composed by Ronald Binge, better known for his 'Elizabethan Serenade'. The version of 'Sailing By' chosen by my predecessor, Tom MacSweeney, who began the programme in 1989, was with Bobby Crush at the piano. 'Sailing By' still regularly features on *Seascapes* on RTÉ Radio 1, however nowadays with the recording by the BBC Concert Orchestra. The current presenter, Marcus Connaughton, whilst in the producer chair since 2002, took the helm as presenter/producer of the maritime programme in January 2010 and introduced a new signature tune. 'The Reel Thing', composed by Simon Mayor and performed by Hilary James and Simon Mayor, taken from their album *Laughing with the Moon*, welcomes listeners aboard *Seascapes* each week on a Friday night at 10.30 p.m.

A special word of thanks to the *Seascapes* team of Niall O'Sullivan and Bryan Fitzpatrick who are pivotal to maintaining the highest standards in the quality of the sound reproduction on *Seascapes*.

Many thanks to our contributing photographers Brian Carlin, Dennis Horgan, David Branigan, Rory Cobbe, Margaret Brown, Eddie O'Hare and David Osborn. We much appreciate the help and encouragement of The Collins Press – Con Collins and Gillian Hennessy.

RTÉ gratefully acknowledges the commitment of our many regular contributors over the past twenty-five years led by our longest serving crewman – Dick Robinson author and lifeboat enthusiast – followed closely by Hugh Oram and Norman Freeman. *Seascapes* is indebted to the support and contributions from Paul Bourke of Inland Fisheries Ireland; Colin Becker of the Inland Waterways Association of Ireland; and Olwen Gill of Inishmore bringing us news of our island communities. Also regulars such as Jim Wilson, naturalist and author; archaeologist Michael Gibbons; Dermot Desmond of the Mission to Seafarers; Dr Michael Martin of the Titanic Trail in Cobh; the Commissioners of Irish Lights; the National Maritime Museum in Dun Laoghaire; Dr Peter Heffernan and his staff in the Marine Institute; Anthony Previte in Clifden; Kieran Devaney; the Irish Sailing Association; Niamh Stephenson and Anna Classon in the Royal National Lifeboat Institution; Gerry Flynn and Gillian Mills of *Inshore Ireland* magazine; *The Marine Times* and *The Irish Skipper*; the Irish Whale and Dolphin Group; Open Water Swimmers and the Master of the Seven Oceans, Steve Redmond; and Fiona Bolger.

Our maritime communities and enthusiasts who make it all worthwhile . . . this is for you, the listener – tight lines and fair sailing.

Bryan Fitzpatrick, Marcus Connaughton and Niall O'Sullivan
(photo by Rory Cobbe)

This book is dedicated to
Daire Brehan
and
John de Courcy Ireland

Galway Hookers (photo by Niall O Regan)

1

Sailing Around Ireland

Paddy Barry

In 2001, Paddy Barry, adventurer/sailor, took his boat Northabout on a 7,800 mile journey to the Northwest Passage. Below he offers a lyrical description of a circumnavigation of Ireland. This was originally broadcast on Seascapes on RTÉ Radio 1 as part of the series of Thomas Davis Lectures.

Would you like to join us in a sailing cruise round Ireland in the Galway Hooker *Saint Patrick*? For fifty years she carried cargo under her red sails in Galway Bay. Now her working days are over, she has an engine and is decked out and fitted for cruising. A 'circumcision' of Ireland, as an old pal used to call it. There'll be three or four of us aboard for the few weeks. We'll go under sail as much as we can, diesel in the tank for when the wind doesn't suit. We'll pull in to places at night, for the odd pint and a bit of music, all dependin'.

It's great on a Friday evening to be leaving the traffic of Dublin behind and then the lovely silence as we turn off the engine and the breeze fills the sails. The wind is from the southwest, which suits, as we go before it and up the Irish Sea.

We round the Baily Lighthouse, and the Kish Light is way outside us. Aren't they very friendly to see, especially at night, when they're blinking away, each with their own special flashes. The Baily flashing every fifteen seconds and the Kish with its double flash. With satellites and GPS instruments now on nearly every small boat, who needs the lighthouses? I like to be able to see where I'm going and it's nice to see high, uncompromising standards. The Commissioners of Irish Lights always did things very well, with their buildings and their machinery. The buildings that housed the three lightkeepers and their families are strong and functional, white-walled with red painted gates and railings. Unfortunately, the lightkeepers are gone – it's all automatic now.

With a nice tide helping us we are past Lambay Island, Balbriggan and Skerries and in a few hours we are crossing Dundalk Bay. Leopold McClintock came from Dundalk. In the way that it was, he was sent off to the British Navy at the age of twelve as a young gentleman of officer material and so he proved to be, one of the Navy's best. In the Northwest Passage then largely unexplored he excelled. The Northwest Passage is the sea route from the Atlantic to the Pacific over the top of the American continent. What made its transit difficult is not the islands, rocks and shallows, but that it is mostly clogged with ice. Even in summer, when the ice of the frozen sea breaks up, the wind blows the ice about and getting through is a lottery.

In McClintock's time, in the 1850s, the middle section, about 700 miles, was as yet untravelled by boat – by non-natives, at any rate. The Inuit who lived there knew it well, then as now.

McClintock sailed there as a British Navy officer. They would overwinter their ships in the frozen sea. Then in spring, when daylight returned, they would pull their sledges over the frozen sea and land surveying and taking soundings through holes in the ice. It was fearsome hard work; the seamen did it for the double pay going with the Arctic voyages. The officers did it to further their careers.

Now the Mountains of Mourne are ahead of us, inshore.

Last year (2001) we went up there. We anchored and went ashore at the very place where McClintock discovered the fate of the lost

Franklin Expedition. Franklin had sailed with two large ships and 129 men, all lost.

We're going for Strangford Lough, where there's a traditional boat festival going on at Portaferry. Old gaff-rigged boats and strong tides, music and porter. Our friend Raphael will be coming on board here, he of the endless observation of all things that grow, fly and swim. 'When the lough goes lazy,' is how he describes the turn of the tide, as we head again for sea.

There are now only two lightships on the Irish coast. One is called South Rock off County Down, and the other is Coningbeg off Wexford. Our boat draws only six feet so we can cut well inside it, to save a few hours. It was near here that in 1989 we lost our good friend Con McCann, who went down with his boat *Connacht*, in a squall. A big tide is emptying out northwards through the Irish Sea, so we'll carry this tide as far as we can.

Belfast Lough inside us, then Larne, Carnlough, the Mull of Kintyre just visible over. You can see why it is that Ulster and Scotland are close in so many ways.

The Ulster champion Cuchulainn got his training in arms in Scotland, said to be from Scáthach, the woman warrior. And by dad, we're making great speed and we get around Fair Head before the tide goes against us. We're into Church Bay in Rathlin Island by evening. There's a new harbour in Rathlin now. Just watch the sandbank as you come along, turn sharply to port between the pier heads, and you're in.

But, like on too many of the new island piers, the construction machinery still lie there amongst the nettles. It was here in a cave in Rathlin that Robert Bruce, on the run, observed the spider doing his 'try, try, try again' stuff. That cave is on the east side of the island, facing Scotland. 'Tis said to be hard to find, but next time we're here we must try to get to it.

Rathlin was our take off point some years ago for Saint Kilda and Iceland. We had desperate weather, but Mike Brogan, in his bunk, off watch, wrote it up in heroic style:

The journey up to Iceland, is worth a verse or two
Strong winds blew from the Arctic, a tester for our crew
But Saint Patrick breasted all the waves, and thro' the seas did run
Twas a lovely sight, goin' up the fjord, we had reached the midnight
*   sun*

Leavin' Rathlin with the west-going tide, the Giants Causeway on North Antrim is not very prominent or visible from the sea. Only for the tourists walking on the shore you'd hardly know it was there.

We're now into 'Drontheim Country'. Accross the north coast, these 'Drontheim' boats were the work horses. Donal McPolin has written a lovely book on them, with gorgeous sketches. These boats have their over-lapping planks, clinker-built, as is the Scandinavian way, which made for lightness, flexibility and strength. The clinker build is found north of a line between Down and Mayo. South of this line all timber boats have their planks butted together, or carvel built as it is called. Four men to a boat, they rowed them and sailed them, fishing for a living, and hauling them up beaches at night.

Happily, like the Galway Hookers and the Achill Yawls, there is now a revival of these old craft, being re-built and sailed but now for pleasure and regatta days. It's great to keep that tradition going.

Past the mouth of the Foyle, Inishowen and Inishtrahull we're on our way to Tory, that rock shelf of an island community off northwest Donegal. Christy Moore and myself once talked about sailing in the hooker to all the Irish islands with a community. We reckoned that there are about 12 of them, depending on which you include. He'd do a non-commercial, unannounced gig. Would have been great craic – but it never came to pass.

Patsy Dan Rogers (MacRuairi) is the voice of Tory, the welcoming man, always on the pier with a welcome and later in the community hall to play the box and to bring out the best in everyone.

Outside the Traonach, the Corncrake fills the night with his croak. The new pier is a great benefit, a life line indeed. This is so for the ferry from the mainland, and for the likes of ourselves too. Down the years before it was built this was an uneasy place for the likes of visitors like us.

Bloody Foreland, so well known, is low and reddish. This is no place to dally, where the North Atlantic storms send the seas crashing in.

So it's nice to get in through the shelter of the islands and drop anchor off the sandy beach at Gola. Beautiful grassy island, its houses are deserted except for a few in summer. Men from Gola sailed on *Asgard*, when she landed guns in Howth. This is the island that gave us the song 'Baidin Fheidhlimi, d'imig go Gola'!

Now bird watchers scan the skies and rock climbers in bright colours hang on Golas cliffs, camping on the island before getting a boat back to Bunbeg on the mainland. The new houses line the coast road. What can you say about them? From the road they seem to clog the place, be it here, Achill or south Connemara. But from the higher ground, Errigal, Ben Lettery or Errisbeg, the landscape looks as it ever did, the white dots below appearing inconsequential.

We'll go on to Arranmore – the Donegal Arran has two r's and is umbilically connected to Scotland by its people who come and go there, and by its 'tunnel tigers' connected to the world. Wherever there are tunnels there are Arranmen.

The big Severn Class Lifeboat here is a 'beaut', 54 feet of muscle and horsepower. God Bless the RNLI and the men and women who crew them.

Rathlin O'Beirne Island, deserted, is next for us. It has two remarkable walls sheltering the grass pathway, which runs from the landing place to the lighthouse buildings. These two walls are seven feet high, of dry walled stone. They must have taken years to build.

Then come the high cliffs of Sliabh League, one of Ireland's three Holy Mountains. These 2,000-feet cliffs are said to be the highest in Europe.

Killybegs, busy and bustling, we'll leave for another day. We need to get across Donegal Bay to Mayo before the weather breaks. That means, once again, having to leave Inishmurray behind. For years we have carried on board the guide book to its monastic remains, in readiness for an informed jump ashore. However its location, deep within the bay, near Sligo, makes the outward westward haul, along the north coast of Mayo, unattractive.

Mayo juts way out westward. This was unknown to the cartographers and navigators of the Spanish Armada. As a result, so many unfortunate Spaniards were shipwrecked on our west coast, some of whom were butchered by our forebears as they came ashore. Erris Peninsula, since the closing of Belmullet Bridge, has to be left inside us. This closing of the opening section of the bridge, and that of some others, shows a great short-sightedness at the time.

At Eagle Island outside Erris I've seen a currach rising and falling, out of sight in the big swell. In it were two men standing nonchalantly working their gear, pots or nets.

You like to stop at Inish Glora, for it was to here that the Children of Lir returned after being changed into swans. As swans they were banished to Derravaragh and the Sea of Moyle for several hundred years. The holding and the shelter south of the island is poor. We visit the monastic remains, sadly in poor order. We then continue down the 10 miles to the shelter of the Inish Gé Islands, Islands of the Greenland Geese. They fly in, each winter, to graze the lush grass of these two islands.

We sailed over to Greenland in summer, to hike along the valleys and climb her sharp mountains. The first time we went in *Saint Patrick* and it took us 21 days to get there. With contrary winds, sea ice and an engine broken down we felt great empathy with the Vikings in their long ships.

In contrast, last year we had excellent wind and it took us only seven and a half days out of Westport to sight Cape Farewell in Greenland. Mind you, it was another three days before we made it ashore because of gales and sea ice.

Back in Inish Gé. The big gale of October 1927, called the Cleggan Disaster down in Galway, decimated these islands. Almost all the men were out fishing in their currachs that terrible night and most were lost.

Inshore of Inish Gé is Broadhaven Bay and further again is Ballycroy Lodge. We anchored and went up the river, a half mile in our dinghy. The lodge, a long two-storied house, is now empty. W.H. Maxwell wrote a book about the summer of 1830 that he spent there. The book is called *Wild Sports of the West of Ireland*. He tells of hunting the eagle, fishing the abundant salmon and drinking the equally abundant claret. Of this he wrote 'that not a farthing of revenue had been paid on it'.

We'll land next on Inish Biggle, untouched by the new prosperity, and by evening we'll anchor off Dugort beach on Achill's north side. To get southward you could go through Achill Sound, if the tides are right, if the Council will open the swing bridge and if the ESB overhead wires are not too low for your mast. On the rare occasion that the bridge is opened, it is a fairly major operation for the men from Mayo County Council. The water supply pipe carried on the bridge has to be uncoupled. Then the winches which swing the steel opening section can be turned. A couple of Hookers did it a few years ago, with Achill Yawl men as our pilots. However it turned out to be a two-day operation. Can you imagine that the weather was so hot that the bridge expanded and got stuck! The next day there were pumps on hand to hose down the steel to cool it. It was great craic, with about six inches of water under our keels and not much more under the wires.

Today our boat is going west around the island. The day is sunny and a few of us are walking the high ridge and sea cliffs of Sliabh

Mor and Croachan, all to meet up at Keem Bay. The Achill men used to hunt the basking shark there. No more; it's holiday makers on the beach now.

It was at Westport last June that we launched the special aluminium expedition boat *Northabout* that Jarlath Cunnane built. We sailed away under Croagh Patrick and bound for Greenland and the Northwest Passage. This passage is an elusive 'one warm line' through a wild and savage land.

As well as trying to get through we were particularly interested in the Irishmen who had gone before us. The names on the charts there speak eloquently of them: McClure from Wexford, Crozier from Banbridge, McClintock we have spoken of, and there even is a Cape Paddy Hennessy – he was up there for seventeen years with the Royal Canadian Mounted Police.

Global warming is real. The Inuit hunters say the summer is longer and the ice is thinner. It freed up for long enough last year to allow us through. Ice-breakers aside, we were the thirteenth boat to do it.

Back to home waters, Clare Island, Caher and Turk with Killary Fjord and Mweelrea overlooking it. The Bens of Connemara now show, as we'll go into 'Boffin for the night, that most musical of islands.

Next day, with heads slightly sore, we go by High Island, former home of Saint Feichin. We sail past the two steeples of Clifden's competing churches and then by Mannin Bay with its sandy beaches and wild flowers in the grass. It's called after the God of the Sea, Manannán Mac Lir.

Next is Slyne Head, or as Gaeilge, Ceann Leime, Headland of the Jumping. You'd need to be some jumper to make it from island to island out there. It's a great thrill to go the inside route inside Slyne Head through Joyce's Sound. It's about two boat lengths' wide, but it has plenty of depth. Even in the lightest of swells, the sea breaks white on the rocks on either side. There's no room for turning back or for second thoughts.

You could spend a month, a summer or even a lifetime between Slyne Head and Black Head in Clare and still not call to everywhere in Galway Bay and Connemara. This is the home of the Hookers, the Báid Mhóra these carried cargo under sail. My own love affair with these boats began in 1966. In Greatmans Bay it was a fine summer's morning. We in our glass fibre 505 racing dinghy were overtaken by a fully loaded Hooker, the *Maighdean Mhara*. Her black triangle of sail carried her silently and powerfully out to Cill Ronan, there to discharge her turf. Two pints for the 'Badoir' and back to Carraroe – a day's work for them, a dream of a boat for me.

Further east are the shallow waters of Kinvara and Galway city, Gallimh, always busy now.

But the summer is passing. In Aran, we shelter out of the wind and rain from the southwest. Later the rain stops, the sky clears and the wind swings to the northwest. We raise sail and go southwards.

We go past the Cliffs of Moher with O'Brien's Castle standing prominent. After Loop Head is the estuary of the River Shannon. Within, Moneypoint and Tarbert ESB stations turn out the power. Further in is Aughinish, locally called 'Treasure Island' during the building of its Aluminium Plant.

Foynes Island was home to Conor O'Brien, he who sailed *Saoirse* round the world in the twenties. Later, in Baltimore, West Cork, he had the *Ilen* built and, with the two Cadogans from Cape Clear, delivered her to the Falkland Islands.

But we're getting ahead of ourselves. Brandon, our third Holy Mountain, is ahead. The islands outside are clear to be seen – Tearacht, Tuaisceart, Vickillaune and Great Blasket.

Tents are now pitched where school children once played. The steep slip still has a few *naomhógs*, where visitors struggle upwards.

Its about three miles over the ridge of Great Blasket to its end, first on grassy track, then on a soft path through the ferns. Barefoot, with sea birds on the cliffs below, there is no finer run.

Walk if you like – you'll see more, and breathe it all in. God in his Heaven, the Skelligs away to the south.

Danny Sheehy once told me that you must always give the *sean fhear* a piece of tobacco when you're passing. This dangerous half-tide rock on the Dun Chaoin side of the Sound is no place for strangers like us to be near.

Further up Dingle Bay is the village of Annascaul, set back from the sea. From here it was that Tom Crean, as a boy, ran off to join the Navy, enlisting in the local coastguard station. Because Tom was 'lower deck', not an officer, he never got all the recognition he deserved. He was a strong, resourceful, willing and humorous man, and was a stalwart in the Antarctic with Scott and separately with Kildare man Ernest Shackleton. He was with Shackleton on the 'small boat journey' and also on the mountain crossing of South Georgia. On Tom's retirement from the Navy, he bought a pub in Annascaul and called it 'The South Pole Inn'. It's there still.

A few years ago five of us did a re-run of Shackleton's Antarctic Escapes after his ship *Endurance* was crushed by sea ice. We were two climbers and three sailors. We built an exact replica of Shackleton's boat (*The James Caird*) and shipped it in a 20-foot container to Tierra del Fuego first and then down to the Antarctic.

We didn't do as well as Shackleton in the boat. In big weather blowing in from Cape Horn, we were turned over, three times, and forced to abandon.

Back home again, we pass the deep bay known as Kenmare River. That's a real misnomer, perpetrated by Lord Kenmare long ago: by calling the bay a river he got fishing rights. After our eighty years of independence isn't it about time that we set this name right?

Dursey Island at the end of the Beara Peninsula is now almost deserted. We'll skip Castletownbere this time and try to get round the Mizen before the weather breaks again.

It's always great to get into Crookhaven, ever since I first bought *Saint Patrick* in there in 1974. I have a lot to thank Billie O'Sullivan for. He kept the boat pumped that summer, when she leaked so badly that he once nearly drowned *inside* of her.

The Carraig Aonar is outside us now, the lone rock. The Irish name is much more descriptive than the name Fastnet.

We could go for either Cape Clear or for Baltimore. Cape Clear, like Blasket, has produced many books, and they say it is a great place to live, but a hard place to make a living.

Before the transatlantic telegraph, Cape was the first place to get the news from the New World. In waxed cloth, the news packages were dropped off inbound ships to waiting Cape Clear boats, there to be relayed by telegraph to Cork and to London.

Baltimore now is a busy fishing harbour. In summer it is alive with holidaymakers and sailors. The ferries constantly come and go, out to Sherkin Iand to Cape Clear Island beyond. To take a break from the salt sea you could go inland towards Skibbereen. Don't take the road, go instead in your boat up the Ilen River. You'll need the tide of course, because the river winds through shallow waters. Woods and pleasant meadows line its banks. The *Skibbereen Eagle* is the newspaper of note in these parts. Even back east as far as Midleton it was always known as being 'first with the news' (that was the transatlantic connection) and it is renowned for its editorial a hundred years ago warning the Czar of Russia that they in Skibbereen were keeping an eye on him.

Going back downriver with the ebb you'll pass Liam Hegarty's boatyard where the Falkland Island vessel called *The Ilen* now is laid up. Gary McMahon and some Limerick friends shipped her back to Dublin some years ago. We re-rigged her, then with seven red sails borrowed from Galway Hookers we sailed her back to Cork and into Baltimore to a great welcome home. This 56-foot boat would make an ideal vessel for any of our coastal towns. She could be used for sail training, corporate outings or even for a few weeks of correctional training for youngsters in need of alternate living styles. Back in Baltimore, the pub The Algerian is a reminder of the infamous Sack of Baltimore. This was in June of 1630. These Algerian pirates were piloted by a man from Dungarvan. It is said that he had a dispute with the fishermen from Baltimore . . .

No less than Thomas Davis wrote:

And o'er each black and bearded face,
The white or crimson shawl.
The yell of 'Allah' breaks above
The prayer and shriek and roar.
Oh blessed God! / The Algerine
Is Lord of Baltimore.

We're on our way again, and going east. We'll go outside Kedge Island and inside The Stags. For years this southwest coast of Ireland was well known to Breton fishermen. Indeed, when we were in Brest for a traditional boat festival in 1992, we heard how the Bretons sailed for Ireland. They would leave on the Spring tide, fish here on the Neaps and then return to Brittany with their catch.

We'll pass Glandore for now. Memory of the loss there last May of *Saint Patrick* is still too sharp.

We'll leave the Old Head of Kinsale, with its big black- and white-striped lighthouse, to the golfers. Access to this headland is now restricted, much to the annoyance of the many who used to enjoy the walk out to it.

If the tide is with us we'll get a good push in the current off the Head. If the tide is running against us, we'll keep in tight to the headland where the run of water is quieter.

Cork, city of Saint Finbarr, yachts, chemicals and pharmaceuticals we'll pass next, and press onward for a short stop at the Great Saltee. The lightship Coningbeg is anchored south of this island. The direction in which she lies to her anchor always tells which way the tidal stream is running.

Or you could go the inside passage between the Saltees and the village of Kilmore Quay, if you like. Of course, you'd need to know where to cross the shallows of Saint Patrick's Bridge. This gravel spit runs from the land out to the Little Saltee. GPS, that little instrument by your chart table that picks up the satellite signal and gives your exact location, makes it all so easy. So different.

It's only a few years ago that we were constantly taking bearings and plotting fixes, trailing logs to give us speed and distance run, and then meticulously recording compass courses made good.

On our longer passages to Spain, or in 1986 going to America, we did it all by sextant. And then all the calculations and that only to get a line of position not even a fix. We don't miss all the constant work and sometimes anxiety of navigation, but we have lost the joy, the exultation of landfall. First you might on your transistor radio start hearing the local radio, then a half day or a day later see the land showing up ahead of you.

In 1987 we first used the Decca, going to the Faroe Islands. In 1990, going to Spitzbergen, we had a Sat-Nav. This gave a position two or three times a day as the satellite passed overhead. By 1993 GPS was in, constant readout for evermore. Even in the small boat *Tom Crean* in the Antarctic, when we were cold, wet and being knocked about, we at least knew where we were!

You always feel safer once rounding Carnsore into the Irish Sea, but it's a false security. The sandbanks of Wexford and Wicklow lie in wait for the unwary. I've heard that Wexford cricketers used to play a game each year on the Blackwater Bank.

The Irish Sea is far emptier now than when the Arklow Schooners plied backwards and forwards to Wales and beyond. They bring our beef, mutton and corn over and the backwards cargo to here was bark for the Irish tanneries or ironmongery.

At Wicklow Head the tide sweeps us north. Soon we're through Dalkey Island, with the lights of Dublin before us.

Solo sailor, David Kenefick (Photo by Brian Carlin)

2

An Epic Voyage

Michael Smith

An extract from Captain Francis Crozier – Last Man Standing? by Michael Smith

Crozier and Ross sailed southwards in a mood of simmering rage. While at Hobart, they had learned that Wilkes and Dumont D'Urville had been active in deepest southern waters, which upset the British sense of propriety. Crozier and Ross, in tune with the chauvinistic doctrines of Barrow, naturally assumed that Britain possessed an inalienable right to explore without the 'interference' of foreign ships.

D'Urville, using Hobart as his base, had found 150 miles (240 kilometres) of new Antarctic coastline between 136º and 142º east, which he named Adelie Land after his wife. Wilkes had the courtesy to write to Ross about his sightings in the region of 100º and 160º east, but Ross, irritated by the unwelcome intrusion, did not reply.

It was decided to drive *Erebus* and *Terror* south along the meridian of 170º east, helped by encouraging recent reports from a British sealing captain, John Balleny. In 1839, only a year before *Erebus* and *Terror* first sailed, Balleny had penetrated further south than either

Wilkes or D'Urville, reaching 69º south, where he discovered open sea.

Ross and Crozier had no reason to feel threatened. *Erebus* and *Terror* were far better equipped than either Wilkes or D'Urville to penetrate the Southern Ocean. Their specially strengthened vessels and their long years of service in the Arctic gave Crozier and Ross a marked advantage over the American and French commanders.

On their departure from Hobart, *Erebus* and *Terror* had set course for the bleak volcanic outpost of the Auckland Isles, about 250 miles (400 kilometres) off the southern coast of New Zealand and the site of the world's largest breeding grounds of wandering albatrosses. It was planned to build an observatory at Rendezvous Harbour, but a major surprise awaited the landing party as they rowed ashore. Two notice boards were discovered with hand-painted records of visits by both Wilkes and D'Urville, who had arrived at Rendezvous Harbour only 24 hours apart. Inside a bottle was a badly soiled note claiming that Wilkes had cruised along an 'Icy Barrier'.

High winds, much like those encountered at the Kerguelens, made the work of erecting the observatory very difficult. After three weeks of struggle, the expedition was relieved when, on 12 December, it pulled away from the island. Before departing *Erebus* and *Terror* left behind an assortment of wildlife – a ram, two ewes, a number of pigs, two goats and some poultry – to provide a source of fresh meat for future visitors to the isolated speck in the vast ocean.

The short, routine trip to nearby Campbell Island almost resulted in disaster when violent winds drove both vessels aground on unseen muddy flats. *Erebus* managed to get free, but Crozier was forced to pump out water and land stores to lighten *Terror*. The ship floated off unharmed at high tide. 'Joy and satisfaction beamed on every face,' Ross remarked as *Terror* was released.

It was an incident which further raised Crozier's stature among his crew. Crozier, though a firm disciplinarian, was always regarded with respect by fellow officers who recognised his first-rate seamanship and close attention to detail.

The first iceberg was sighted two days after Christmas and even weathered Arctic hands such as Crozier and Ross were amazed at the enormity of the huge monolithic islands of ice that loomed out of the sea and dwarfed *Erebus* and *Terror*.

Icebergs in the Antarctic are much different to those that Crozier and Ross had encountered so many times in the Arctic. While the Arctic bergs are more conical and resemble small floating hills, the giant Antarctic bergs are mostly huge, flat slabs of ice with steep perpendicular cliffs. Some Antarctic bergs have measured 100 miles (160 kilometres) in length, but are more typically between 300–1,000 feet (100–300 metres).

Erebus and *Terror* pushed further south in wild weather, and crossed the Antarctic Circle on New Year's Day 1841, a feat marked by the issuing to all hands of more winter clothing and extra grog.

Erebus *and* Terror *in the Antarctic ice*

Billy, the pet goat, was given lashings of port wine and staggered around the quarterdeck to the amusement of the crews.

The mood on board was optimistic. On 6 January, Crozier transferred to *Erebus* for a light-hearted party to celebrate Twelfth Night and then invited Ross to finish off the evening with more drinks on board *Terror*. The revelry came to an abrupt halt, however, when one of *Terror's* sailors fell overboard and had to be rescued.

The ice became more dense and tightly packed as the ships pressed further south. Before long, the horizon to the south was filled with an unbroken field of ice and *Erebus* and *Terror* faced the choice of seeking a way through the pack ice or retreating to warmer waters and abandoning the mission. The ships drove on southwards, looking for gaps in the ice.

The ice belt around the Antarctic continent presents a formidable barrier to ships. No vessels had entered the pack ice in this area before, and sailing ships, who were at the mercy of the region's ferocious winds, were particularly vulnerable to collision.

The pack encases the Antarctic continent like a girdle, extending in width from 350–1,800 miles (560–2,880 kilometres) and it prevents ships from reaching the mainland for much of the year. Leads of open water, which are sprinkled with large and dangerous blocks of floating ice, open and close under the influence of currents and strong winds. Ships entering a lane of open water can find their entry and exit routes suddenly closed off by the constantly moving ice.

Crozier and Ross sailed south in strong winds, anxiously searching for inviting lanes of open water. The ships frequently sought shelter in the lee of colossal icebergs that towered over their masts. Suddenly the line of retreat was cut off when strong gales blew from behind the ships and the ice closed together.

With little option but to continue south, it was decided to ram the ice with the bows of the blunt-nosed ships. *Erebus* went first, followed by Crozier in *Terror*. Sometimes, the ships managed to break through, but often they came to a sudden halt as the ice re-

Mount Erebus

fused to give way. On the ice, startled penguins scuttled alongside in wonderment.

For several days, the ships dodged and weaved among the leads, with visibility often obliterated by bouts of fog and white-out conditions caused by swirling snowstorms. The ships frequently lost sight of each other. On deck, the men fired muskets or rang bells to make sure they did not get too separated.

The decks and sails were covered in a ghostly shroud of ice and the sea spray froze as it fell on the ships. Steering half-blind and surrounded on all sides by heavy ice, the ships crept southwards, on constant alert for icebergs. Sometimes, they brushed alongside a giant berg and men used poles to prevent a heavy collision.

On occasions, *Erebus* and *Terror* came to a standstill, waiting for the moment when a gap would appear between the giant bergs before slipping quickly through the opening. At midday on 9 January, the fog suddenly lifted to show the ships in open, ice-free waters. 'Not a particle of ice could be seen in any direction,' Ross gleefully reported.

Ross and Crozier, ably assisted by a skilled crew, had achieved one of the greatest feats of navigation in the history of exploration. Taking two small wooden sailing ships through the Antarctic pack ice for the first time was an achievement to rank alongside the outstanding exploits of men like Ferdinand Magellan and James Cook. It was a feat put into full context 70 years later by Roald Amundsen, the finest of all polar explorers, when he described the journey as the 'boldest voyage known in Antarctic exploration'.

Writing in 1912, Amundsen applauded Ross and Crozier:

With two ponderous craft – regular 'tubs' according to our ideas – these men sailed right into the heart of the pack, which all previous polar explorers had regarded as certain death. It is not merely difficult to grasp this; it is simply impossible – to us, who with a motion of the hand can set the screw going and wriggle out of the first difficulty we encounter. These men were heroes – heroes in the highest sense of the word.

From *Captain Francis Crozier – Last Man Standing?* by Michael Smith, published by The Collins Press, www.collinspress.ie.

3

Caring for the Radar

Norman Freeman

Norman Freeman, a frequent contributor to Seascapes, is a former radio officer and the author of Seaspray and Whisky: Reminiscences of a Tramp Ship Voyage.

Radar, that marvellous navigational aid and safety system, comes into its own on dark nights at sea. The screen, with its revolving cursor, shows up the coastline, rocky islands, nearby vessels and other potential hazards.

Today's sophisticated radar sets rarely break down. However, before the era of transistors and microchips, radar sets had an array of valves, capacitors and resistors, some of which could fail. They were part of the complicated innards of the large transmission and receiver unit. This was usually housed in a metal hut above the bridge-deck of those ships whose owners could afford to install what was then a very expensive system.

One of the most common faults was the radar going off tune. The echoes of land and other ships would be replaced by aggravating, swirling lines of orange dots. Up in the radar hut, the radio officer would find that the needle of the tuning dial was swinging this way and that instead of being steadily upright at 90 degrees. By twiddling various knobs, he would try to coax the needle back to its proper position, thus restoring the picture on the viewing unit below on the bridge.

I first saw this vital little indicator when studying for the Radio Officer's Certificate (Second Class) in the College of Science and Technology in Kevin Street in Dublin

Our instructor, Mr Blennerhassett, emphasised to us: 'Radar is an expensive and delicate piece of equipment. It has to be treated with immense care.'

The next time I saw a tuning dial on a radar was on my first ship. We carried the generally reliable Marconi Mark IV radar. However, at around midnight, as we were traversing the reef-hazardous passage between the African mainland and the islands of Zanzibar and Pemba, the radar went off tune. The captain, who was given to fretting at the best of times, sent down for the Chief Radio Officer.

The Chief came staggering up. He was furious at being disturbed while drinking in the first class lounge and trying to make advances to a well-seasoned lady passenger.

When we climbed up to the radar hut and removed the front cover on the big unit we could see straight away the needle of the tuning dial swaying back and forward. The Chief, with his nail-bitten fingers, began to twist and turn some of the associated tuning knobs. But the needle had a will of its own. To his fury, it did not respond.

I soon became aware that the Chief knew almost as little about the radar as I did myself. He effed and blinded. In the hothouse of the radar hut and the heavy equatorial heat the sweaty, gin-smelling odour from his bloated pink body was overpowering. 'That old bollix will blame me,' he shouted, referring to the captain, whom he hated.

All his efforts to retune came to nothing. His rage got the better of him. He sat down on the steel doorstep, braced himself by holding on to the sides of the hut. 'I'll get you, you hoor you,' he shouted and smashed his heels against the unit. There was a tremendous bang. The whole unit shuddered. Then, low and behold, we saw the tuning needle quiver and return to its steady, upright position. Perhaps one of the many finely-balanced components responded to the jolt.

We scampered down to the bridge. When the Chief looked into the viewing unit he could see the coastline of Zanzibar.

The Captain approached in the semi-darkness. 'Don't tell me you've fixed it, Sparks?' he said sarcastically.

'Oh, it was a complicated fault, sir, but I think I've managed to put it right,' replied the Chief, with the air of someone whose knowledge and expertise had passed a severe test.

The Jolie Brise celebrates its centenary off the Fastnet (photo by Brian Carlin)

4

Fastnet '79

Gerald Butler

Gerald Butler, one of Ireland's last lightkeepers, was featured on Seascapes on RTÉ Radio 1 in March 2013. Below he describes the tragic 1979 Fastnet yacht race, and his role as lighthouse keeper on Fastnet Rock.

The famous Fastnet yachting competition first began in 1925 and runs every two years over a course of 608 nautical miles. The race starts at Cowes in the Isle of Wight in England, rounds the midway point at Fastnet Rock, returns to England through the south side of the Isles of Scilly and finishes at Plymouth.

When the 1979 Fastnet race began on Saturday 11 August, I was on duty as an assistant keeper on the Fastnet Rock lighthouse with the principal keeper, Reggie Sugrue, and a temporary keeper, Louis Cronin. Two tradesmen were also working there at the time.

As keepers on Fastnet, our official role in the race was to maintain radio listening watch and to pass on any messages that were not being acknowledged by the intended receiver, as well as providing an aid to navigation by keeping the lighthouse beam shining.

As was traditional, once the participating yachts came into view, the Fastnet keepers would note their sail numbers and times of passing. Then, we would radio the information to the keepers at Mizen

Head and they would telephone the data to the race organisers in Cowes, as well as to the *Cork Examiner*.

On that fateful Saturday in August, 306 yachts, with 3,000 competitors on board, from 22 countries, set sail from Cowes to begin the race. Weather conditions were ideal, with reasonable winds and calm seas. The BBC radio shipping forecast broadcast at 1.55 p.m. predicted, 'South-westerly winds, force 4 to 5, increasing to force 6 to 7 for a time.'

On the following Sunday morning, a dense fog closed in around Fastnet Rock. Rolling fog is a regular occurrence in that particular part of the coastline, especially if warm southerly winds are present.

On Fastnet, we issued weather reports to the Irish Meteorological Service every four hours, as an aid to their forecast. We gave the direction and strength of the wind, the air temperature, the rise and fall of the sea, as well as the amount of cloud in the sky. Only certain lighthouses provided this service. Also, at Fastnet, as well as at every lighthouse, we recorded weather conditions every hour for a fog watch and also every four hours.

When keepers signed off from a watch, they recorded the barometrical pressure, by noting whether it was high or low and by measuring the pressure in inches. On that Sunday, conditions were still good and ideal for the race.

On Monday, the fog cleared at 8.45 a.m. and the wind registered at southerly force 3. A woman named Mrs Good rang Fastnet Rock and asked me if she could come out to the rock by boat to watch the yachts circling the lighthouse. I warned her against it, as the wind had begun to freshen and the fog had cleared very quickly. Both conditions together indicated that the weather was about to change for the worst. Around 2.00 p.m., the wind shifted to south-south-east and increased to strength 4.

On Fastnet, we kept a close eye out for the yachts. About 4.00 p.m., as the wind shifted again to southerly force 4, the first of the vessels sailed into view and began to round the lighthouse. These yachts were huge and rated among the biggest of the fleet. They would have gained great ground as the freshening, south-easterly winds would have blown them forward and increased their pace.

As evening approached, the winds grew stronger. Our radio on Fastnet broke down. Luckily, an Irish Lights helicopter happened to be in Castletownbere and delivered a new radio to the rock, which was a radio telephone transmitter and receiver, in medium frequency, with a range of about 150 miles. While we awaited the new radio, we kept contact with the keepers on Mizen Head by telephone. Once the new radio arrived, we resumed radio contact with them straight away.

At 6.00 p.m., the wind shifted back to south-south-east and increased to force 6. A small, wooden, pleasure craft sailed out to Fastnet from Crookhaven to observe the yachts rounding Fastnet. The weather deteriorated rapidly and the wind strengthened. The sea raged and the rise and fall of the waves varied between 10 and 15 feet. Standing on the balcony of the Fastnet, I watched the small vessel for hours through my binoculars as it tried to take shelter on the rough sea. It was the only boat in sight. Since the passing of the first, large, race yachts, no other yacht had reached the Fastnet, which suggested that the remainder lagged far behind the leaders.

Fastnet Rock

I continued to watch the small boat as it struggled on the sea. At first, it sailed under the Fastnet. Then, it drifted eastwards and headed towards Cape Clear Island, about three miles east. But I was unsure if the craft was actually in difficulty, as it seemed to be keeping its head up against the weather. At 8.00 p.m., the wind increased to gale force 8 and it began to rain. Conditions deteriorated further.

At 10.00 p.m., the lights of the small vessel disappeared and the boat went out of sight. I became alarmed and immediately contacted Baltimore Lifeboat by telephone. The secretary's wife, Eileen Bushe, answered the call. She listened attentively to my concern. When I requested to have the lifeboat launched to search for the vessel, she said that it was already on the ocean, as a boat with an RTÉ press crew on board had failed to return to Schull at the expected time. On that fateful night, the members of the lifeboat crew who took to the seas were: Christy Collins, coxswain; Pat Harrington, acting second coxswain; Michael O'Connell, mechanic; John O'Regan, assistant mechanic; Noel Cottrell, second assistant mechanic; Paul O'Regan; Dan Cahalane; and Kieran Cotter. Although the lifeboat The Robert scoured the ocean in search of the small vessel, it failed to find the missing boat.

As the lifeboat began making its way back to Crookhaven, some of the racing yachts sailed into view near Fastnet. By now, the storm was raging and the sea thrashed 55 feet high against the entrance door of the lighthouse. We locked up and battened down all our storm doors. We had no fear for our own safety, as we had experienced much harsher conditions in winter time. But we were now becoming increasingly concerned for the 3,000 competitors in the race, many of whom had small vessels, no radios and may have been inexperienced in sailing on enormous seas in stormy weather.

In the lighthouse, we had an Aldis lamp, which we used for Morse code by light at night and which could throw a bright beam over a distance of several miles. Now, we used it to read the sail numbers on the yachts as they rounded Fastnet. We sent the information to

Mizen Head lightkeepers by radio and they forwarded it to Cowes by telephone.

Sometimes, when we shone the Aldis lamp on the yachts, a massive wave battered against the rock and blotted out our view, allowing us to see only a huge volume of water, sweeping forcefully right over the rock, leaving merely the top of the tower visible. We took no notice of the onslaught and continued to shine our light on the yachts.

At 11.00 p.m., conditions worsened. The sea rose higher and higher and battered against the rock at a height of 80 feet. The wind reached strong gale force 9. As the yachts continued to round the Fastnet, the crews battled hard to control their boats. The number of people on each yacht varied, depending on the size of the boat. On average, crews probably numbered between six and nine.

At midnight, the wind shifted again from south-south-east to southerly and increased to storm force 10. At 15 minutes past midnight, we started sounding the fog horn. To the mariners struggling for their lives on the tempestuous sea, its high-pitched blare must have sounded like a siren from hell.

On Fastnet, we listened to the radio on the distress frequency 2182kcs, to which all ships at sea are constantly tuned. Many yachts were in serious difficulty. Some were capsizing in the far-off distance, east of Fastnet. But many of the boats had no radio and no means of communication. They could only rely on other nearby vessels to report their distress.

On the distress frequency, some of the yachts between the Scilly Isles and Fastnet broadcasted a May Day Relay, which is a call for help for another capsized yacht. But many of the mariners who saw their competitors in difficulty were unable to assist them. Being at the mercy of the mighty sea and violent storm, they too would have capsized if they had stopped to help.

As we listened on Fastnet to the distress frequency, we picked up information from many of the struggling crews, not only about their own yachts, but also about other boats. We heard that people were clinging to the sides of their boats on the mountainous ocean, that many yachts were turned upside down, while other boats showed no sign of life. Some vessels were rolling 360 degrees. Even the world-class yachts were in serious trouble, with some pitch-poling, flipping end over end. Although the voices of the distressed mariners sounded agitated, they communicated their cries for help with clarity. They gave the name of their yacht and sail number, as well as an accurate description of their position and the state of their vessel.

When we shone the Aldis lamp on a yacht, it lit up the entire deck and surrounding water, which was in extreme turmoil and breaking high over the decks of the yachts. Crew members were struggling to walk on heaving decks, trying to keep their balance, as they strove to trim their sails, to control their boats, while the person at the helm tried to turn the boat. Many of the yachts were only a quarter of a mile east of Fastnet. As they attempted to round the lighthouse, they kept a long way west of the rock, to avoid being foundered. But their task was tough, as they were at the mercy of the vicious, swirling wind and tumultuous sea.

At 1.35 a.m., a Cork yacht named *Regardless*, owned by Corkman Ken Rohan, put out a distress call when it lost its carbon fibre rudder. The yacht was positioned about three miles south-east of Fastnet Rock and had been fancied to win its class in the race until it got into difficulty. As the boat lost control, the crew lowered its sails and streamed ropes from the stern to keep the yacht's head onto the seas. The southerly wind continued to lash at force 10.

After spending hours searching for the small missing vessel, the Baltimore lifeboat, *The Robert*, which had begun its route to Crookhaven, set off west to save *Regardless*. The yacht had been drifting north-north-west. On seeing the Fastnet light, the lifeboat crew took their bearing from it. They knew they were south-east of the lighthouse, probably three or four miles away, but could not be certain of the exact distance. At the time, navigation equipment was unreliable and the crew had to rely on a Radio Direction Finding, which is a navigation system used to identify a radio source. As there were at least 15 yachts in the area at the time, battling against the storm, it was almost impossible for the lifeboat crew to distinguish one yacht from another and to identify *Regardless*. By then, the Irish naval ship, the *LE Deirdre*, was standing by the yacht in distress, as it happened to be patrolling the area. Its presence helped the lifeboat locate *Regardless*. Once the lifeboat arrived, *Regardless* cast off its ropes, to avoid fouling her propellers, and *The Robert* began towing her towards Baltimore, with a crew of nine on board. Along the way, the tow was lost five times.

Only yards off Fastnet, close to the rock, we could see Hugh Coveney's yacht, *Golden Apple of the Sun*. Ron Holland, the designer of the yacht, was among its crew, as well as Scotsman and three-time Olympic yachting medallist Rodney Pattisson. The yacht sliced its way through a narrow passage of water that opened up after a wave struck the rock, fell back again and met up with an incoming wave. The vessel was so near the lighthouse that we could almost reach out and touch it. Years before, when I was lobster fishing with Pat Joe Harrington, our neighbour at Galley Head, he explained to me about this calm strip of water, saying an old fisherman had told him that if skilled sailors kept their wits about them in stormy conditions, they could sail on this narrow channel, as it was known to be a safe passage.

By now, the vicious sea was breaking up high over the top of Fastnet Rock, hammering at a height of 90 to 100 feet and causing the tower to sway. Building material tied on to the side of the cliff, about 80 feet up the rock, was ripped asunder. At that stage, I was due to go off duty, to try and get a few hours sleep. Knowing that we had a long night ahead and that we needed to be on top of the job, it was important that each lightkeeper took a nap, even if only for a few hours. As I lay in my bunk bed, I could hear stones rolling below on the ocean floor and banging relentlessly against the tower. The southerly wind continued to batter at storm force 10.

After I resumed watch at 2.00 a.m., a group of four yachts came into view. Due to the strength of the mighty ocean and storm force winds, they failed to turn at the Fastnet. Instead, they were forced to head for Crookhaven, to turn their yachts near land. Many of the other yachts abandoned the race and veered to ports along the south coast of Ireland, such as Baltimore, Ballycotton, Cobh, Cork Harbour, Crosshaven and Kinsale, while some headed for Wales. *Finndabar*, owned by Patrick Jameson, a commissioner at Irish Lights, abandoned the race just off Kinsale, while *Morning Cloud*, whose skipper was the former British prime minister Edward Heath, lost its rudder and headed for Cork Harbour. Later, Mr. Heath recalled his ordeal: 'It's an experience that I do not think anybody would want to go through again willingly. It was a raging sea with enormous waves and one of them picked us up and laid us on our side.'

In the early hours of the morning, we stopped reading the sail numbers, as we felt the powerful glare from the Aldis lamp was blinding the crews and hindering their struggle. At 3.00 a.m., the wind shifted up to the west and continued up to storm force 10. The westerly wind hoisted the waves up to about 40 feet at sea and in excess of 100 feet on the rock.

All through the early morning hours, the race participants battled on, with the westerly wind still howling at storm force 10. Around 6.00 a.m., the wind shifted into the north-west. Shortly afterwards a massive search and rescue operation got underway, co-ordinated by the Shannon Rescue Co-ordination Centre and the Plymouth Rescue Control Centre. Over 4,000 rescuers were summoned, among them the Royal Navy; the Dutch Navy; the entire Irish Navy; tugs; tankers; trawlers, including French trawlers; commercial ships; a fleet of RAF helicopters and RAF Nimrod jets, Irish Sea Rescue Services; and lifeboats from RNLI England and the south coast of Ireland, including crews from Courtmacsherry, Youghal, Valentia, Dunmore East and Ballycotton, with *The Robert* continuing to play its part. Most of the rescuers would have been called in by British Coast

Radio. The British Air Force flew over, having been summoned by Landsend Radio, a coast radio station set up to handle shipping telephone messages. They air lifted many of the crews in difficulty. By coincidence, the Irish Navy happened to be on patrol when the yachts got into difficulty and contacted their naval base at Haulbowline in County Cork to summon the rest of the fleet.

Many of the damaged vessels were escorted into ports, such as *Silver Apple*, which called for help after its steering broke, and was led into Cork Harbour by the *LE Deirdre*. The crew of *Alvina* took to a life raft and had a narrow escape, as their vessel smashed to bits shortly afterwards. Hugh Coveney and his entire crew were airlifted to safety by an RAF Lynx helicopter after the yacht's rudder snapped in colossal waves and the ten men on board squeezed into a life raft. The crew of *Hestrul II* was also airlifted.

As day was breaking, I saw a small yacht, about 30 feet in length, come into view from the east, which was the direction from which many of the distress calls came. It had hoisted its storm jib, which is a very small sail on the bow. The yacht moved extremely fast. In an instant, it spun around and headed in the opposite direction, confirming yet again the powerlessness of the yachts against the storm. Eventually, the yacht was able to correct its course and round the Fastnet.

About 8.00 a.m., *The Robert* landed *Regardless* and its crew safely at Baltimore. Then it headed off to search for the 55-foot *Marionette* and its crew of twelve, which, like *Regardless*, had lost its rudder. The yacht gave its position as south-east of the Stag's, a few miles from Baltimore. By the time *The Robert* located *Marionette*, it had drifted 25 miles south of Galley Head lighthouse.

At 10.00 a.m., the wind began to decrease to strong gale force 9. In the next hour, the wind shifted to west-north-west and blew at force 8. Around 1.00 p.m., the wind dropped to force 7. At 3.00 p.m., it shifted to west and then fell further to force 6.

Gerald Butler at Fastnet

Midway between Land's End and Fastnet, at least 125 competitors, whose yachts had been caught up in Force 11 violent storm strength gusts, were picked up by rescuers.

On the mainland, Richard Bushe, the secretary of Baltimore Lifeboat, organised ambulances and arranged a supply of dry clothes for the survivors. The crew of *The Robert* had worked tirelessly and helped survivors for 36 hours non-stop, longer than any other lifeboat.

Back at Plymouth Harbour, worried relatives and friends of the sailors who had not returned stood on the pier, gazing far out to sea, over the waters of the English Channel, waiting anxiously for the return of their loved ones.

Gradually, the extent of the horrific disaster began to unfold. Sadly, 15 of the competitors had perished in the monstrous storm. Six of the lives were lost because safety harnesses broke. The remainder drowned or died from hypothermia. The deceased sailors were named as Paul Baldwin, Robin Bowyer, Sub Lieutenant Russell Brown, David Crisp, Peter Dorey, Peter Everson, Frank Ferris, William L. Fevre, John Puxley, Robert Robie, David Sheahan, Sub

Lieutenant Charles Steavenson, Roger Watts, Gerrit Jan Williahey and Gerald Winks.

Of the 306 yachts in the race, 25 were sunk or disabled, among them *Magic, Polar Bear* and *Charioteer.* Abandoned yachts included *Allamader, Ariadne, Billy Bones, Bonaventure, Callirhaex 3, Fiestina Tertia, Gan, Kestel, Maligawa III, Tarantula, Trophy* and *Tiderace IV.*

One of the survivors, Matthew Sheahan, who was only seventeen at the time and a crew member on his father's yacht, *Grimalkin,* described losing his father in the storm: 'One of the crew had realised my father was in a very bad way and needed to get out from under the boat, and he had cut my father's safety harness to free him. As I stood up and looked up, I could see a body, face down in the water. We were drifting away from it. There was absolutely no question in my mind that it was my father. The worst thing was that he was upwind of the boat and the boat was drifting downwind. Had it been the other way round, we could have got the life raft or something to go downwind and help pick him up. But upwind in those conditions: impossible.' He also described the impact when the yacht capsized: 'We were thrown out of the boat. Sometimes it would just be rolled over onto its side and catapult the crew into the water. Other times it would roll completely over and come up the other way. Worse still was when it was pitch-poled, when the boat actually does a cartwheel. The bow ploughs into the wave in front and the back gets lifted up by another wave.' He added that the waves were the size of buildings.

Dónal McClement, a navigator with the Royal Air Force and skipper of a seven-man crew sailing in the RAF class-4 yacht, *Black Arrow,* recalled his ordeal: 'I made a decision about 2.00 a.m. that even if a boat was next to us, there was nothing we could do as we would be risking our boat and our crew in helping them. We saw flares going up so we knew people were in trouble but there was no way we could get to them. I was lucky that I had a crew that were very experienced and used to discipline and leadership. Others just didn't know what hit them.'

Over the coming days, Valentia Radio broadcast the names and sail numbers of missing yachts. On Fastnet Rock, we checked our records to see if any of these were entered as having passed Fastnet. We were able to give the sail numbers of some of the yachts that passed and were still passing. However, our records were incomplete, as we had switched off the Aldis lamp in the early hours of Tuesday morning.

Following the disaster, the media spotlight focused on Fastnet Rock. Reggie, the principal keeper, was interviewed on RTÉ radio, during a 9.00 a.m. news broadcast, and gave a detailed description of the sea disaster.

Although the storm had erupted out of the blue, people were now pointing the finger and looking for someone to blame. Doubt was cast on the weather reports issued by the lightkeepers at Fastnet Rock. We submitted our weather reports in their entirety to the headquarters of the Commissioners of Irish Lights at Pembroke Street in Dublin. We were duly commended for our accuracy and received a letter of appreciation on behalf of the Commissioners of Irish Lights in September 1979 stating: 'I am pleased to convey their thanks and appreciation for observations and communications with the sea and air rescue services, which, in the best tradition of this Service, helped greatly the success of the sea and rescue operation in your area.'

The Royal Ocean Racing Club, which had organised the race, received heavy criticism, especially in relation to its failure to call off the race when the weather seriously deteriorated, as it was argued that many competitors kept on racing for the honour of the race, instead of running for a port. Together with the Royal Yachting Association, the Royal Ocean Racing Club immediately commissioned an official inquiry into the disaster. By setting up the inquiry rapidly, both organisations hoped to preempt any official government inquiry and to show that sailing was a sport that could govern itself responsibly. The inquiry cleared the Royal Ocean Racing Club of any blame.

In the aftermath, new regulations were introduced to limit the number of yachts competing in the Fastnet race to 300. Also, it became compulsory for all yachts to be equipped with a VHF radio and for safety harnesses to have a locking device. Qualifications for entry to the competition were also introduced. Furthermore, a new strapping to airlift seafarers in difficulty was developed, consisting of a strap for around the legs and a strap for around the waist. In 1983, restrictions on electronic navigational aids were lifted.

The Fastnet yacht race of 1979 left an indelible mark on my mind that remains to this very day. In the wake of the tragedy, I received many moving telephone calls, one of the most poignant being a call from Mrs Good, the woman I had advised not to sail to the rock. She phoned to thank me for the warning.

The tragedy stands as the worst offshore racing disaster and the largest rescue operation ever in peacetime Europe, while the weather conditions of the time were described as the deadliest storm in the history of modern sailing.

Years after the race tragedy, while I was on duty on Mizen Head during the Cork Dry Gin Round Ireland Challenge yacht race, I was having a cup of tea with members of an RTÉ outside-broadcast unit, who were waiting to film the yachts circling Mizen. When the conversation switched to the tragic Fastnet race of 1979, I told them about the little vessel I had watched for hours until its light disappeared. They said that they were the crew of that very vessel, as they had sailed to the Fastnet to film the race. They were unaware that *The Robert* had been launched to search for them. Their vessel had made its way safely back to Crookhaven. All of them survived.

From *The Lightkeeper: A Memoir*, by Gerald Butler with Patricia Ahern, published by The Liffey Press, www.theliffeypress.com

Dun Laoghaire lifeboat off Dalkey (photo by Dave Branigan/Oceansport)

5

The Royal National Lifeboat Institution

Dick Robinson

Dick Robinson, the longest serving contributor to Seascapes, is the author of
Valentia Lifeboats: A History

The Royal National Lifeboat Institution was formed on 4 March 1824 at a meeting in the City of London Tavern. These premises were on the site now occupied by the Brown Shipley Building in Bishops gate London EC3. A plaque on the wall of that building states: 'On this site where formerly stood the City of London Tavern, The Royal National Lifeboat Institution was founded as a voluntary body at a meeting held here on the 4 March 1824, presided over by the Archbishop of Canterbury, Dr. Charles Manners Sutton.'

The Institution was the brainchild of Sir William Hillary, Bt. Hillary, a Yorkshire man, was a man of many talents and ideas. However he found himself in difficulties financially – having lost his own and his wife's fortunes, as well as his marriage. He betook himself to the financial safety of the Isle of Man. It was here he got involved with the local lifeboat and performed many outstanding rescues. He issued a pamphlet on the merits of a National Lifeboat

Institution for (1) the preservation of human life from shipwreck – the first and great object of the institution; (2) the assistance of vessels in distress; (3) the preservation of vessels and property, after people have been rescued; (4) the prevention of plunder; (5) succour and support for the rescued; and (6) rewards to the rescuers, provisions for widows and orphans. He proposed the same volunteer ethos that is alive and well in today's service.

By the 1840s the institution was in a sad state. Many boats were unmaintained and fishermen used their own. In the 1850s two men – the Duke of Northumberland, who was appointed president, and Richard Lewis, a barrister who was appointed secretary – set about rebuilding the institution. Records of events before these men arrived are sketchy and vary with the tome one reads. As Barry Cox, Honorary Librarian with the RNLI for some 20 years points out in an article for The Lifeboat Enthusiasts Society: 'Many people also strongly believe that the RNLI became "Royal" after the granting of the Royal Charter in 1860. The minutes of the committee of management clearly record that on 20th March 1824, King George IV awarded the title of "Royal" to the Institution, and so it has remained ever since.'

Originally, the lifeboats were powered by oar and sail. Various boats were built to meet the requirement of particularly difficult local standards. One of the most peculiar must be at Port Isaac, in Cornwall, where anybody building a house had to do so 'above lifeboat level' to allow the boat to be pulled through the streets to launch. The ropes cut into the walls and notches were clearly visible on some buildings.

In the 1880s steam lifeboats were built, six in all, but by 1904 the move to petrol-driven boats was in place. The power behind the lifeboats was changed to, and now remains, diesel. If one were to look at the old rowing lifeboats and the motor boats built up until 1974 the hull was the same almost elliptical shape. Non-self-righting boats were the majority of the craft. After the *Longhope* and *Fraserburgh* lifeboats were lost the decision was taken that the boats would all become self-righting.

Like every other aspect of life the 1960s changed the RNLI. The two big changes were the introduction of the inshore lifeboats in 1963 and the first 'fast' (15 knot) all-weather lifeboat in 1967. In 1972 the Atlantic class inshore lifeboats vastly enhanced the lifesaving capacity of those craft. In 1971, the Arun class 18 knot lifeboat was built and in 1996 the 25 knot Severn and Trent class boats were introduced. Today the Tamar class and Shannon class are the 'brand leaders'. The RNLI also operates Hovercraft in several locations.

The lifeboats are really about people – people who save and people who are saved, people who help and people who are helped, and people who never even saw the sea but put money in a bucket held by people who are anxious that the RNLI will have the necessary funds.

On 7 August 1994 it was a beautiful day, seas were calm, a north easterly breeze force three to four was blowing and the weather and visibility was good. Nevertheless at 2.30 p.m. a call came from the Canadian flagged yacht *Quan Ying 2* of Boston that she had suffered engine failure. She was thirty miles southwest of Valentia. She had a fuel shortage. Under command of Second Coxswain Richard Connolly, the lifeboat *RNLB Hibernia* embarked twenty gallons of fuel and put to sea. They reached *Quan Ying 2* at 5.30 p.m. They found the sole crew member exhausted and looked after her.

The lifeboat crew helped to refuel and clean up the yacht. Seventy-nine-year-old Mary Harper, who had sailed single-handed from Boston, insisted on carrying on under her own power. Once satisfied that all was well with Mary the lifeboat returned to her station. Ms Harper sent a donation of $200 to the station.

In Ballycotton, on a plinth, facing towards the Daunt Rock, is the former lifeboat *Mary Stanford*. Here she will be restored. She tells the story of one of the most famous rescues in the history of the RNLI. On 7 February 1936 the lifeboat put to sea from Ballycotton in seas that were truly horrendous. Over the next 76 hours the crew endured the savagery of the sea. She was to be away from the station for 76 hours of which 49 were spent at sea. It took six runs alongside the madly heaving lightship before all nine crew were saved. All the crew were completely exhausted and cold and had salt water burns; the coxswain had a poisoned hand when they returned to Ballycotton. In the 63 hours from when they left Ballycotton until they landed the survivors at Queenstown they had only three hours sleep.

In Poole, where the RNLI is headquartered, the chief executive, senior management team and staff run all the managerial and financial and operational. Here too is the Lifeboat College where volunteers and crew attend for world class training. On the site now construction is proceeding apace on a new site which will facilitate the building on site of the RNLI lifeboats.

Heretofore boats were built on contract by various boatyards. Changes to the Royal Charter, which had been granted in 1860, led to major changes which allow the RNLI to build their own boats. It also allowed for lifeboats to operate in the Thames and in inland waters such as Lough Derg, Lough Ree, the upper and lower lakes at Enniskillen and on Lough Ness.

The RNLI also provides a flood rescue service as well as Sea Safety Advice.

The RNLI has lifeguard patrols on some 200 beaches. It is also involved in international development to provide knowledge, equipment and training in tandem with local agencies to prevent drowning in Bangladesh, Brazil, the British Virgin Islands, Cameroon, Kenya, Philipines Senegal, Tanzania, the Gambia, Uganda and Uruguay.

In 2013, lifeboats rescued 8,384 people, 325 lives were saved, and lifeguards were called to 19,594 incidents. Lifeboats rescue 23 people every day. In addition, 8,826 lifejackets were checked by experts and there were 15,795 incidents where first aid was needed. Lifeboats launched 8,304 times and 8,826 lifejackets were checked.

There are silent people who rescue others,
from shipwreck and flood and fire,
And vocal people who tell mankind
What it should and should not desire,

Those who work with the silent people
Know that always and nevertheless,
Attention turns to the vocal people,
The political and economic people,
The projected and personally purposeful people,
Except when there's sudden distress
– Patrick Howarth

Nearly 200 years since Sir William Hillary wrote his pamphlet on the Isle of Man the organisation has survived, improved and grown to international proportions. Volunteers now are both men and women. Some are born to sea and seafaring; some have no experience but are trained to a high level of competence. Whether they are facing a rescue as a lifeguard or on a Severn class lifeboat in Rosslare or Valentia or Aran Islands, Ballyglass or Arranmore or Portush, they will have been taught the necessary skills.

Having the bottle to come to a lifeboat station or a lifeguard's hut and say, 'I'll do it – I'll go', cannot be taught. That has to come from the heart.

Therein is the spirit that makes the Royal National Lifeboat Institution the great organisation that it is.

Dog watching the gaelgoiri depart

6

Ireland's Western Islands

John Carlos

An extract from Ireland's Western Islands – Inishbofin, The Aran Islands, Inishturk, Inishark, Clare & Turbot Islands by John Carlos

This book is a celebration of the islanders of Inishbofin and the Aran Islands: Inis Mór, Inis Meáin and Inis Oírr, County Galway. It includes the islands of Inishturk and Clare Island, County Mayo, and also honours the people of Inishark and Turbot Island, County Galway, who were evacuated from their islands by the Irish government in 1960 and 1978 respectively.

The work reflects on disappearing traditions and culture in a society increasingly consumed by materialism, information technology and celebrity culture. The sequences, which suggest a form of narration, draw on many elements to create a unity of opposites: people, wild flowers, youth, landscapes, home, religious icons, work, seascapes, animals, fish, rocks, love and loss. People and nature are intricately woven to portray their relationship with the islands, and the complexity of their lives therein.

The book is not an attempt in any way to define the islands or their people, but rather, to preserve a memory of the islanders and their homelands. Although the work spans almost fifty years, the photographs barely touch the surface of such a rich and diverse culture.

The population of our offshore islands has dwindled from 35,000 in the 1800s to fewer than 3,000 today. Between the 1950s and 1970s, several communities off the western seaboard were displaced from their islands, resulting in the destruction of their culture and identity.

The lack of adequate investment in employment incentives, even during our economically buoyant times, has drained the population on islands such as Inishturk. In 1985 there were thirty pupils in the island's National school; in 2014 there were three.

There are few temples or shrines honouring Irish islanders. There are, however, a myriad of memorials dedicated to their folk and fishermen lost at sea. Apart from earlier visits to Inishbofin since 1976, the main thrust of the work was undertaken there and on the surrounding islands from 1992 until 2011. The photographs in Aran were made at various intervals from 1965 until 2013.

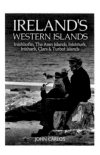

From *Ireland's Western Islands – Inishbofin, The Aran Islands, Inishturk, Inishark, Clare & Turbot Islands* by John Carlos is published by The Collins Press, www.collinspress.ie

7

Ireland's Emigrant and Convict Ship Trail

Michael Martin

Michael Martin is a graduate of UCC and University of California Berkeley. He is originally from Dublin and served for 23 years in the Navy. After retirement he established the Titanic Trail Guided Walking tour in Cobh which still operates today. His most recent publication is entitled RMS Lusitania: It Wasn't and It Didn't (Dublin, 2014) which addresses the common narrative of the circumstances surrounding the sinking of the ship during the First World War. The essay below is one of six Thomas Davis Lectures that aired on Seascapes on RTÉ Radio 1.

In the middle of Cork Harbour, Sunday evening, 28 May 1848, a man considered by some to be a hardened criminal, by others a patriotic hero, flung himself down on a bed and broke into a raging passion of tears. He wept uncontrollably. His surroundings comprised of a prison cell sparsely furnished with just a bed, a table and chair and a nightstand. It overlooked a lonely courtyard inside the walls of the fortress on Spike Island in the middle of Cork Harbour. The man was John Mitchel, one of the group set up by

Emigrants Leaving Ireland – engraving by Henry Doyle, 1827–93

Thomas Davis and others in the early 1840s who became known as the Young Irelanders. He had been a contributor to their paper *The Nation* when it was first published in 1842 and had later in 1848 launched his own paper known as the *United Irishman*. He had been highly regarded and had practiced law. But on this day he was confined and alone, a convict on an island that was to become synonymous with convicts and with transportation.

There are seven islands in Cork harbour – Spike, Rocky Island, Haulbowline, Hop Island, Fota, Little and Great Island. Each has its own distinctive story to tell. Where else on earth would you get seven islands in such close proximity that were overlooked by pre-Christian cairns, that hosted sixth century monasteries, twelfth century military posts, fourteenth century governors, eighteenth century penal settlements, military annoury magazines, castles, keeps, Martello towers and the magnificent nineteenth century neo-gothic architecture of St. Colman's Cathedral. These islands have witnessed the ravages of invasion, absorbed the tears of tragic famine, been tread upon by young grey-faced soldiers destined for war in foreign parts. They have heard the wails of those dispatched in chains to distant prisons and felt the ray of hope in emigrant expectations.

Cobh is situated on the largest and most important of these islands. Its winding streets cling to ancient cliffs and hills. The whole town overlooks the grace and majesty of what is said to be the second largest and most beautiful harbour in the world.

The history of Cobh, or Queenstown as it was known during British rule, includes its role as an important military port where hundreds of thousands of soldiers, sailors and Defence Department officials of the British establishment were stationed.

During the First World War an American fleet of 93 ships came too, and over the years hundreds of shipping company clerks and executives operated the shipping line companies that flourished when Cobh was a hub of transatlantic travel.

Millions of emigrants, many fleeing political or economic oppression and even starvation, fled through Cobh. Presidents of Ireland, and of the United States, Queen Victoria and Laurel and Hardy have passed along the streets.

Cruise liners still visit making their way through the narrow entrance of the harbour. Navigating around Spike Island to squeeze between Haulbowline and Great Island, they berth at a deepwater quay that was honed out of bedrock and developed in 1882, disgorging passengers, who are often, in the rush of modem tourism, left by the tour operators blissfully unaware of the heritage and history of Cobh and Cork Harbour and of its timeless links with events that shaped peoples and nations throughout the world.

Cobh and Cork Harbour is an area of maritime fascination with stories of Phoenicians invading, 32 boats filled with 30 men each under the command of a colourful Phoenician prince 1,200 years before Christianity reached us. Their ancient gravesite or cairn on Currabinny hill in the southwest corner of the harbour a reminder of their pre-Christian period presence.

I am captivated by the idea of Christian monks on Spike Island in the sixth and seventh centuries going about their simple daily tasks in devotion and humility.

The arrival in Cork Harbour of the Vikings must have been traumatic. Plundering, pillaging and raping their way up to and into Cork City. Leaving and then returning to eventually open up new sea lanes and routes enabling better trade and commerce.

King Henry sent men. Sent with the endorsement of the world's only ever English Pope, Adrian IV, they recognised immediately the value of the harbour and didn't leave for eight centuries.

The Spanish Armada sailed up and down the south coast outside the reach of the cannon batteries, placed in the 1540s, on either side of the only entrance to Cork Harbour. Had they got past those cannons it might have changed the course of Irish history.

Cobh, and the magnificent harbour it graces, has played host, in the days of sail, to those ships that probed and searched out new lands. That crossed angry oceans and rounded fearsome capes. It has been occupied by the military and naval might of a past world power. It has witnessed the tragic drain of entire generations of emigrants, millions of them leaving from there, setting out with hope and determination, waving goodbye from creaking decks as they slipped away to find a better life and a prosperous future.

But of all the categories of invader, traveller, visitor or migrant that passed through Cork Harbour, one group didn't come by choice but by compulsion. Their time in the Harbour was spent in dreaded

expectation of a lifetime of separation from normal life, of deprivation and fear.

They were the convicts. Those awaiting transportation. As early
as 1597 Queen Elizabeth I had passed a law which would provide
for 'Rogues, Vagabonds and sturdy Beggars to be banished from
this Realm'. Any such rogue returning to the Realm without permission would be hanged. Those with death sentences hanging over
them were ideal candidates to be sent to the new world for use by
the emerging colony. In the early 1600s entrepreneurs of the new
American colony requested convicts for slave labour and so, in the
British establishment at least, the idea of slavery as a contingency of
justice began. Cromwell transported many Irishmen to the planta-
tions of Jamaica and Barbados in the mid-1600s. Then in 1717 a new
law was passed which extended the use of transportation to those
guilty of minor offences. The periods were set at that time at seven
and fourteen years.

By the 1750s the rapid growth of population in Ireland and Britain was causing widespread social deprivation with a corresponding
increase in the incidence of petty crime. Bulging prisons and increasing costs on the State were to be relieved by the transportation of
petty offenders to the American colonies.

In 1776 those who were seen in Britain as the 'ungrateful American' colonists declared independence and went to war. It was a long
and bitter conflict but the surrender of the British Army in York-
town in 1781 heralded American independence. Transportation to
America was now finished. These world events would have an impact on Cobh, would add a chapter to its history that is chilling in its
breadth of cruelty and despair.

In May 1787, under the command of Captain Arthur Phillip, the
first fleet set sail from Portsmouth intending to land at Botany Bay
and colonise Australia. Among the ships of this fleet were 733 convicts, some younger than 15. After a voyage of eight months Botany
Bay was thought too inhospitable in which to land and so the fleet

sailed on to Sydney Cove where the first vestiges of a colony and an open prison were started.

In 1788, the British Government officially announced that Australia was to be the new penal colony and four years later transportation of convicts began from Cobh and Cork harbour to New South Wales. Spike Island became the base where some of the convicts were prepared for transportation. This island in Cork Harbour had had its fortifications upgraded by the then ruling British Government as a result of fears of a future American or French invasion. Started in the early 1790s, the labour force was made up from convicts who would have been sent to America had independence not been achieved there.

Across the harbour the sound of clinking metal on stone was heard as quarrying took place and a causeway was built to move stone from Haulbowline to Spike for the building of the new fortress. Metal on metal was also heard across the swift running waters of the harbour as bleeding ankles and torn feet dragged heavy leg irons over rough terrain. That sound was to be followed by the horrors of transportation as convicts were sent to Australia to provide forced labour on another continent. In 1803, the first convicts were sent to Van Diemen's Land and were used to build the Port Arthur Prison, which was to become one of the most feared destinations among the rumour-ridden convict community.

From the 1790s through the following 60 years, over 30,000 men, women and children were transported from Cork Harbour and Spike Island to Australia and Van Diemen's Land.

Where today children play on the small beach at Cuskinny Bay near Cobh, their watching parents probably do not realise that dark and forbidding prison hulks lay there at anchor in the past. The moans and the suffering of convicts, chained like animals, could be heard ashore. They lay in squalor and fear awaiting their fate: to be transported to the other side of the world.

From the hulks anchored there, imprisoned men, women and children were transferred to the transport ships under a cruel sentence often convicted of some of the pettiest crimes imaginable.

John Morgan from Drogheda was 60 years old. He was married with two children and was sentenced to seven years transportation for stealing four chickens. He died, still a prisoner in Port Arthur, Tasmania at the age 84, never having been re-united with his family.

Thomas Cahill from County Tipperary was only 12 years old when he was transported for seven years for vagrancy. Because of his age he was sent to Point Puer, an island prison for boys off Port Arthur. It was infamous for the number of suicides of young inmates there.

At the age of 13 William Mulhall got seven years transportation for stealing a pair of shoes. Towards the end of his sentence he was further charged with the offence of smoking tobacco and for this his sentence was extended. In his despair he tried to hang himself. This too was deemed an offence and he was sentenced to suffer more years in the hell that was transportation.

Many tortured souls were to take their convicted bodies through Cork Harbour but some never left on the dreaded convict ships. They died in awful conditions as they waited to be transported. A windswept area on the southwest corner of Spike Island was used as a convict burial ground, but even in death convicts were to be badly treated. They were deemed unfit to be buried in hallowed ground and so were interred nameless. Some of those dying on the creaking prison hulks at anchor are said to be buried in mounds visible in the marsh behind Cuskinny strand.

If a convict survived the hulks and the hard labour they were eventually placed on the transport ships anchored and waiting in the harbour. Dark holds were filled to capacity with chained bodies. There was no lighting, no sanitation facilities, and when all were aboard the holds were battened down. Below, terrified convicts, many who had never been to sea, only knew their voyage had begun when the darkened interior began to rise and fall with the motion of the sea. Ships like the *Britannia* that sailed from Cork in 1796 bound for Sydney was recorded as being one of the most depraved, brutal and cruellest voyages ever undertaken. Disease, torture, starvation and cruelty resulted in the death of one in every six men on board!

Cork is said to be the second largest natural harbour in the world after Sydney, Australia. I'm not sure if that's true. Having criss-crossed San Francisco Bay I'm a bit cautious about the claim, but nonetheless the comparison is appropriate because the connections with Sydney are strong.

The thousands who left these shores in chains looked finally and longingly at the rolling hills and wooded headlands of Cork Harbour before being shoved below decks on the transportation ship into the squalid surroundings that would be their hell for the next few months. They ached at the prospect of separation and departure. The next rolling hills they would see would be in Sydney Cove when they were unloaded, still in chains, now emaciated, half-starved and some literally dying.

But even in the life of convicts there were class differences. The other class of convicts were those that were deemed to be gentlemen.

One group that found themselves new additions to the family of convicts in the 1840s were the Young Irelanders. Inspired by the philosophy and passion of their founder, Thomas Davis, they grew frustrated with the continuing failure of peaceful efforts to bring about Irish independence. Thomas Davis died in 1845. Three years later John Mitchel established the *United Irishman* newspaper as a channel for encouraging insurrection. A call to arms that the paper printed resulted in the Young Irelander leadership (John Mitchel, William Smyth O'Brien and Thomas Francis Meagher) being charged with sedition. A month later new laws were passed and Mitchel was charged with treason. Smyth O'Brien and Meagher were acquitted of sedition but Mitchel was found guilty and sentenced to 14 years transportation.

He was immediately sent by sea from Dublin to Cork Harbour and imprisoned on Spike Island to await the arrival of the vessel that would take him to Van Diemen's Land. Describing his arrival on Spike, Mitchell wrote: 'We came to anchor opposite Cove and within 500 yards of Spike Island, a rueful looking place, where I could discern, crowning the hill, the long walls of the prison, and a battery commanding the Harbour.' He was escorted to his cell which was just beside a little courtyard not far inside the gates of the fortress.

Of his surroundings during his short stay on Spike he wrote: 'In this courtyard there is nothing to be seen but the high walls and the blue sky. And beyond these walls I know is the beautiful bay lying in the bosom of its soft green hills.' The cellblock and courtyard that Mitchel describes can still be seen on Spike, although a different type of prisoner, sentenced for offences by Irish courts, occupies a jail on the Island today and it is a lot more comfortable than in Mitchel's time.

Within days Mitchel was to leave Spike and set sail for Bermuda on his way to South Africa and finally to the dreaded Van Diemen's Land. During the first months of his voyage, and unknown to him, the leaders of the Young Irelanders were again arrested after a failed attempt at rebellion and they too were transported.

Van Diemen's is today known as Tasmania and is Australia's only island state. Its history and indeed that of all of Australia is inextricably linked to the countless Irish convicts that were sent there during the period between the 1790s and the 1860s. The Botany Bay that Captain Cook described in glowing terms on his voyage of discovery in 1770 turned out to be unsuitable for settlement. Today, however, it is in use for visitors of another sort entirely. Sydney International Airport is located there now. I wonder how many people realise when they are landing there that it is the very place that was intended for vagabonds, thieves and convicts!

In Tasmania, Mitchel was permitted to live as a gentleman in a location decided by the governor, provided he gave his word he would not try to escape. This was in stark contrast to the arrangements on Spike Island. He agreed and was sent to a small town called Bothwell towards the central highlands of Tasmania. It would have been very foreign to any Irishman there. The terrain, the vegetation, the wildlife and even the seasons were very different to back home and very different to his last images of Ireland as he sailed out past Roches Point in Cork Harbour. He ached for his family and initially rented accommodation over a shop in the tiny village where he was sent. The little shop, known as the Bothwell Stores, is still trading!

He was required weekly to present himself for roll call at a specified location in the town and in this way the local magistrate was kept informed of his presence in the prescribed area. Today Bothwell is still a small town with about 300 inhabitants.

Many of them take pride in their knowledge of John Mitchel. On a recent visit there they were delighted to show me the actual places where he spent his days. He eventually leased a cottage and 200 hundred acres just outside of the town, and brought his wife out to share their life together in Tasmania.

While he was in Bothwell, his Young Irelander colleagues Thomas Francis Meagher and William Smyth O'Brien had arrived at Van Diemen's Land. Meagher agreed to the same conditions as Mitchel and was sent to live on the shores of the remote Lake Sorrel further north than Bothwell. Even today it takes a two hour hike through the bush off an unpaved road to get to the ruins of his cottage near the lake. He lived there with two servants in the midst of the Tasmanian wilderness.

Smyth O'Brien, on the other hand, refused to give his word on the matter of attempting escape and as a result was assigned to Maria Island off the east coast of Tasmania. In planning to go there I had visions of finding a remote and hostile place, windswept and dreary. Instead, it became evident as we approached it by ferry that Maria Island was a very beautiful place indeed. It did not have the grey walls or the treeless landscaped shape of Spike Island.

Instead, a dominant forest-crowned mountain protects the northern side of the island from the ravages of the Southern Ocean. The island is blessed too with a crescent-shaped golden beach that bathes in the southern hemisphere sunshine for most of the day. There are cliffs, meadows and ancient trees, all with an abundance of native wildlife. William Smyth O'Brien was provided with his own cottage there. Despite the island's beauty he passionately missed the company of his own class and was not permitted to mix with others on the island anyway. He wrote: 'To find a gaol in one of the loveliest spots formed by the hand of nature in one of her loneliest solitudes creates a revulsion of feeling I cannot describe.'

Smyth O'Brien didn't stay on the island long. Australian historians refer to a perceived scandal in the making when O'Brien took an interest in the governor's daughter. He was sent to Port Arthur. This was the most dreaded place of all and was usually reserved for those convicts found committing second offences after they arrived in the colony.

Situated on the southern tip of Tasman peninsula, this huge prison complex had no outer walls. There was nowhere to go for escapees except into the wilderness of the bush. Those convicts who did try to escape down through the years usually had their bodies found in the hostile bush that surrounded the area.

The peninsula was a perfect place to build Port Arthur. At one point it narrows to about 200 yards at a place called Eagle Hawk neck. Just in case anybody did make it this far the authorities had a steel chain strung across the stretch with a dozen fearsome dogs snarling and ready to devour anyone who approached.

Port Arthur itself was a large complex. It had the main prison, a dockyard, a hospital, a lunatic asylum, two churches and a military area where soldiers were housed. Again, William Smyth O'Brien was given his own cottage. He was also refused permission to mix with any of the other prisoners. A large wall was built around the cottage itself, which deprived him of even the sight of other human contact. His cottage was on a hill overlooking the bay, but like Mitchel on Spike Island he could only imagine the scene outside. Had he been able to look upon it he would have seen the main prison complex beneath him with two islands just offshore. One was called Point Puer and was a prison island for children of 14 or less. Tales abound of young boys joining hands and jumping off the small cliffs of the island committing suicide pacts. The authorities always denied these. The other island is simply known as the Isle of the Dead. It is where hundreds of convicts were buried, again with no headstones and no dignity.

Staff at the Port Arthur visitor complex were recently struck with the similarities between the arrangements on Spike Island in Cork Harbour and the Isle of the Dead.

O'Brien found it increasingly difficult to endure his isolation. A prison doctor feared that his mental health was suffering. He eventually agreed to the terms of his ticket of leave and was released from Port Arthur to take up residence in a town called New Norfolk in the Derwent Valley north of Hobart. He had freedom of movement there and, more importantly, the ability to mix socially which he had missed so much.

Meanwhile, in a remote location called Interlaken, straddled between Lake Sorrel and Lake Crescent where their two jurisdictions bordered each other, Meagher and Mitchel met secretly. In a shepherd's hut there they plotted their escape. Unlike thousands of others they were successful and escaped to America.

Meagher left his wife Catherine behind in Tasmania. She was heavily pregnant and planned to follow him after the child was born. He was never to see his son at all and never saw his wife again either. The infant, Hemy Emmet Fitzgerald, died aged four months. Catherine returned to Ireland and while awaiting her trip to America she fell ill and died. The child's grave lies beside the small Catholic church of St Johns in Richmond, Tasmania.

Both Meagher and Mitchel fought in the American Civil War. Having led an Irish brigade at Friedricksburg, Thomas Francis Meagher was awarded with the Deputy Governorship of Montana! He died later in 1867 in mysterious circumstances on a riverboat on the Missouri. O'Brien was later pardoned and went back to Europe to live in Paris. Mitchel lived out his life in New York, controversial and opinionated to the end of his days.

Like Cobh and Cork harbour, the hills, forests and natural formations of Tasmania bare testimony to historical events and human endeavour and suffering. The crumbling walls of Port Arthur, the lonely beach on Maria Island, all hold direct connections with our heritage as do the walls of Spike Island prison and the piers and streets of Cobh.

Direct connections like these are there to be explored. They are our heritage. They should fascinate and inspire us. The walls that stand on Spike Island in Cork Harbour are the very same ones that were built with the trembling hands of Irish convicts. They are part of us and we of them. Places such as America and Australia were moulded by the sweat and suffering of these people. Today we live in better times. Our circumstances are much improved, but somewhere in the world now as we speak there are people going through the agony of oppression, the injustice of wrongful separation. We have our harbour, its history and its islands as a living reminder of where we came from and who we are. Let us cherish them.

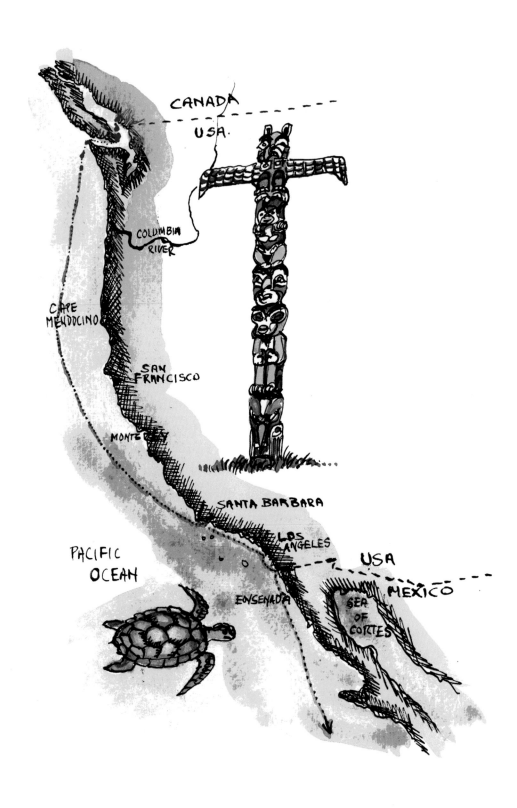

8

The Rescue of the Molly B

Pete Hogan

Dublin-based artist Pete Hogan appeared on Seascapes in January 2013 to describe how he built his own sailboat, the Molly B, and sailed it down the West Coast of America through the Panama Canal and across the Atlantic to Achill Island. Below he describes how early in the voyage it almost came to an end until he was rescued by the US Coast Guard off the coast of Santa Barbara.

> '*Hark now hear the sailors cry*
> *Smell the sea and feel the sky*
> *Let your soul and spirit fly into the mystic.*'

The recommended route for going south in a yacht from the strait of Juan de Fuca is to get well offshore. Harbours to the south are few and usually have bars, which must be crossed, guarding them. In addition, the great Columbia River discharges into the Pacific 120 miles to the south and can cause a disturbance over a wide area. Because of the time of year and without a motor, I intended to stay well offshore.

In grey overcast weather I got underway, sailing out into the Pacific past Cape Flattery and Tatoosh Island. Here I sailed through a pod of grey whales as they cavorted in the shallow water off the island. I took it as a good omen. The wind was in the southeast, no good for going south, but I could sail offshore, which was what I wanted to do.

For three days Molly B stood to the west. I was sick as a dog. I suspect it might have been something I ate which caused it, rather than seasickness, or a combination of both. I could only lie on my bunk and change down sails as the wind increased. The boat crashed out offshore, west into the Pacific for perhaps 150 miles. I had little idea where we were and cared less. The main sail, furled badly on the boom, damaged itself by rubbing holes through the cloth. I didn't care. The wind increased. I hove to for a day. A passing ship slowed down to check me out. I waved to them and they passed on. In the end, exhausted and despairing of getting a favourable wind, I said 'enough' and turned and headed back towards the east and land. Five days after setting out I found myself back off Cape Flattery again and ready to put back into Neah Bay for a regroup and rest. Suddenly the sun came out and the wind went around to the north. I managed to hold down a bowl of porridge. Things were looking up. I hoisted the torn mainsail and we scudded off to the south.

For the next ten days I sailed down the coasts of Washington, Oregon and California. At times I made good progress, when the wind blew from the north and northwest. At other times I made less than ten miles a day. Sometimes Molly B was able to self-steer but more often I had to sit at the tiller and heave to at night. There was one southerly gale where I had to heave to for a day and one northerly blow when I could raise the double reefed main and surge off to the south.

The traffrail log would not work and this was a big loss. It would jam and spin itself into a hopeless mess. The sky was too overcast for celestial navigation most of the time and I was not very practiced at working out sights at this early stage in the voyage. The log would have been a good check on my dead reckoning.

It is worthwhile describing in some detail the chain of events which followed. Sixteen days out from Neah Bay my celestial navigation put Molly B off Point Arena, which is 100 miles north of San Francisco. I ran on to the south expecting to pick up Point Reyes with its powerful light marking the northern approaches to San Francisco. I was in sight of the shore and all next day expected to see Point Reyes. A further day's run to the south and I began to realise that I was lost and that I was south of San Francisco bay. Tired and confused I blamed several factors for my predicament: the boat had to heave to each night and drift out to sea, I could not distinguish with certainty any of the shore lights because there were so many of them, and the faulty traffrail log made dead reckoning inaccurate. But lost I was and in sight of shore.

I sailed on and came to a prominent headland by evening but could not positively identify it even when night fell and its powerful flashing light came on. It was more than likely Pigeon Point to the south of San Francisco. I hove to for the night and drifted south. In the morning the headland was out of sight and I was far offshore. I sailed towards the shore. A noon sight put Molly B off Monterey Bay. The shore consisted of rocky rugged cliffs. Things were starting to fit into place. I had seen the famous coast of Big Sur often on TV and movies. I ran south along the cliffs all day watching the cars on the road above. By evening I reckoned Molly B to be off Cape San Martin and hove to for the night.

The next day, I further confirmed my position by a noon sight and by reading my pilot book, looking at the land and picking out the features. By evening I was identifying the Minutemen rocket silos on the foreshore to the north of Point Arguelo mentioned in my pilot book. Santa Barbara, 40 miles around the point, was the obvious place to head for. 'I will drop anchor in Santa Barbara tomorrow after the toughest sail of my career,' I said to myself. I was tired and confused. It was now the 18th day of the trip. I had expected to be at sea for 10 days.

I hove to for the night. I tacked *Molly B* around at midnight and hove to on the other tack to avoid getting too far offshore. As the dawn broke and the wind died away I could see Point Conception, the dividing line between Northern and Southern California. The sun came up. I could see oil rigs in the distance. It was going to be a scorcher of a day, I thought, as I discarded woolly socks and jumpers. I hauled out my battered sun hat as *Molly B* rounded Point Conception.

There was a strong current sweeping out of the Santa Barbara Channel. I could see this by *Molly B*'s lack of progress along the shore. I headed inshore to avoid the current and to look at the fancy ranch houses that dot the bald green slopes.

By midday the sun was high in the sky, the wind calm and the sails flapping about. I had been on the tiller since before dawn at 4.30 that morning. I ate a huge pancake breakfast and felt dozy. It seemed safe enough to take a nap. I lashed the tiller and dropped the main sail, leaving the genoa and mizzen up. I did not anchor because I thought it might be too deep and did not want to lose one of my

nice shiny new anchors. I went below and lay on one of the bunks. I estimated that *Molly B* was about two miles offshore, though from what happened next it might have been less.

Not long after slipping into a deep weary sleep I was roused by the gentle lurch of the boat bumping on something. As I stuck my head out the hatch, it happened again only a little harder. As I looked around I could see that the boat was running straight up on the shore. It was too late to do anything. The hull bumped gently twice again as *Molly B* surged through the surf like a surfboard. Then as she connected firmly with the shore, *Molly B* slewed around broadside on to the waves, keeled over on her side and started to pound on the rocky ledges.

Things looked grim. In fact, it looked like the end of the road for the voyage of the *Molly B*. We had run ashore at a place called Coho, which is just east of Point Conception and, ironically, a recommended anchorage. There was virtually no wind but quite a swell running, a thing quite common on the coast of California. The *Molly B* was grounded on flat rocky ledges that extended from the beach below some low cliffs. There did not appear to be any houses nearby.

It is easy now to describe the scene calmly but at the time things were confused and happening at breakneck speed. *Molly B* became firmly lodged on the flat sandstone rocks, beam on to the incoming waves. There were deep fissures in between the rocks, through which the water rushed and gurgled. Each incoming wave would take the hull of the boat and, pivoting it on the keel, crash it down on the inshore side, the rocks pounding a hole in the starboard side. The outgoing wave would have the reverse effect, pivoting the hull back on to its other side, the masts and the rigging describing a broad arc through the air. Then the next incoming wave would begin the process again. There was confusion everywhere, ropes and sails and bits of equipment tossed all over the decks and cabin. I had to hold tight to a mast or rail to stop myself being thrown off the deck.

At first the hull bounced clear when on top of the waves and I thought that if I could get an anchor out into deep water I might have a chance of hauling the boat off. I launched the 9 foot dinghy from its position on top of the cabin. The next incoming wave filled it and capsized it. I jumped into the water. I could stand on the giant flat rocks, the water up to my waist. I had to be careful not to get caught under the hull as it came flying across with the waves. I brought the dinghy ashore through the surf thinking to bail it out and try again. But I could see that it was useless. *Molly B* was stuck fast, a majestic and frightening sight as only such disasters as shipwrecks can be. The swell whooshed in relentlessly and the hull pivoted on its keel each time and pounded down on the rocks. The masts, swinging like a giant inverted pendulum were still standing. I was amazed that the rigging was taking the strain.

A girl with two kids came up the beach. In true Californian style she empathised with me, telling me that she knew how bad it must feel to crash my boat! She said the nearest phone was in a house some miles away. She said she would go and call the Coast Guard.

I went back on board. I was convinced now that the boat was doomed. The water was starting to slosh about above the floorboards. The hull would fill with water before anything could be done to save it while it still floated. Then it would be smashed to smithereens in the surf and on the rocks. I gathered a sail bag full of valuables. The radio, my camera, the sextant and the log. A sleeping bag for if I had to camp on the beach.

Just then I noticed a small boat offshore, bobbing about beyond the line of surf. There were two people on board and they were shouting and waving at me. I waved at them and shouted back. 'Call the Coast Guard,' I yelled. 'Call the Coast Guard.' I assumed they had a radio.

We continued shouting at each other but the distance was such that proper communication was impossible. They seemed to be telling me to get on my radio but did not realise that *Molly B* did not have one.

I got out the longest rope on board – over 200 feet long. I attached it to the bow of *Molly B* and swam out through the surf towards the small blue boat. I was still quite far from it when I came to the end of the rope. I shouted for them to come in a bit closer. It seemed to me to be deep enough. The men in the boat attached a line to a large buoy and floated it off in the water. There was not wind or waves enough to make the buoyed rope move in my direction. It was off to the side. I was getting tired and cold as I treaded water at the end of my rope. I started to fear that I might drown. I abandoned the rope and swam back to *Molly B*. Just hoisting my exhausted body back on board was difficult. My knees could hardly support my body; they had turned to rubber.

Molly B was still pounding heavily on the starboard side and seemed to have been moved up the beach into shallower water. The hull would only now pivot when a particularly large roller came sweeping in. Below in the cabin the mess was indescribable, water sloshing everywhere freely.

I began to think that the Coast Guard was the only hope of being pulled off the beach. I looked out at the small blue boat beyond the surf and thought that even if I did get a line to them the boat could not be powerful enough to pull *Molly B* off. 'Probably a couple of amateur fishermen out for an afternoon's fishing,' I thought. 'They won't understand the problems of what's involved here.' Their boat

looked very small, only a speedboat. I shouted vainly out to them to get help.

There was nothing much I could do except hang on to the pounding *Molly B*. I started to tidy up the mess of ropes and sails. I dropped the genoa and mizzen sails, which were still up. The surf continued to roll in. I was resigned to the loss of the boat and my dream. It was all over unless the Coast Guard arrived.

Then, like an angel sent by the Lord, in through the surf swam one of the men. 'Hello. Hello, matie,' he said with the accent of a London bobby. 'What's going on here?' He hauled himself on board. Called Ray and wearing a wet suit he explained that the blue boat called *Moki* could not come any closer as it had a deep propeller which might get damaged in the shallows. Ray had swum in with a line as far as it would go and left a buoy on the end of it between *Moki* and *Molly B*. Together we joined two anchor lines and Ray swam back out with them and connected with the line to Moki.

Moki turned and faced out to sea, the line attached to her stern. Slowly the strain came on the rope. *Molly B* was still bouncing clear of the bottom on the crest of large waves. *Moki* revved up, her stern digging into the sea, exhaust smoke swirling up and her bow lifting as the strain came on the rope. Slowly the bow of *Molly B* turned and faced out to sea. As each roller swept in and lifted the hull clear of the rocks she started to move, slowly at first. With much yelling and whooping from the crew of *Moki*, like cowboys at a rodeo, off bounced *Molly B* and slid out through the surf into deep water.

It was getting late in the afternoon and dusk was starting to fall. The two boats tied alongside and cleared their lines. Jon the captain and owner of *Moki* introduced himself. He was an abalone diver and Ray was his helper. They were very excited to have pulled the hull off the rocks, as was I to be rescued. Jon was kept busy talking on his radio to the Coast Guard who were following proceedings blow by blow. 'There's a coast guard cutter and a helicopter on its way,' said Jon. I could not have been in better hands.

In the cabin of *Molly B* the water was well above the floorboards and the hull was visibly settling in the sea below the waterline. I started pumping with the bilge pump. Ray came aboard and helped. We took it in turns. The 30 gallon a minute bilge pump plus a bucket could just keep up with the flow. 'The chopper will bring a pump,' said Jon. We tried stretching a sail over the hull around the keel to slow the intake but it did not have much effect. I had read about that trick in my Hornblower books.

Jon was in contact with the Coast Guard, which was on its way. As the chopper approached, the two boats separated. They would drop the pump on to *Moki* as there were no masts or rigging to obstruct things. Just as darkness was falling the chopper arrived. It was a powerful sight as it hovered over the little blue boat 50 meters away from *Molly B*. It reminded me of movies about the Vietnam War. There were lights blazing, strobes flashing, rotors roaring, turbines whining and a circle of waves whipped up on the surface of the

water. The crew of the chopper, in white helmets and dark shades, peered down inscrutably, like spacemen.

Two pumps, packed in large steel drums, were lowered on to the deck of *Moki* and the chopper sped off into the night back to Los Angeles. *Moki* moved back alongside *Molly B* and all three of us lifted

one of the pumps on board. 'They give you two in case one does not work,' explained Jon.

It took us some time to get the petrol-driven pump working. We had to prime it using a kettle. Then, once working, it cleared the bilge in a matter of minutes. By now it was dark.

'Let's go,' said Jon.

We rigged a towline from *Molly B* to *Moki*. I found a replacement for the tiller on *Molly B*. The tiller had snapped when the boat hit the beach. We set off for Santa Barbara, which was 30 miles away and *Moki's* home port.

Ray stayed on board *Molly B* as it needed one man to steer and another to operate the pump every 15 minutes or so. It took five hours to reach Santa Barbara, *Molly B* surging along at her hull speed of about six knots. *Moki*, a light displacement 25 foot planing speedboat with a powerful inboard/outboard motor, could normally expect to make about 25 knots, so progress was slow by her standards.

We reached Santa Barbara at 2 o'clock in the morning and tied up *Molly B* in the travel lift of the boat yard. 'See you in the morning,' said Jon as he took off in his truck. I catnapped for the rest of the night, operating the Coast Guard pump every half hour or so to keep *Molly B* afloat. Tired and in a dazed, zombie-like state, I realised that the boat had been saved. What luck! Snatched from the jaws of Davy Jones's Locker. The voyage wasn't over yet.

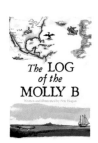

From *The Log of the Molly B,* by Pete Hogan, published by The Liffey Press, www.theliffeypress.com

Trawlers off Dunmore East (photo by Marcus Connaughton)

9

Fishing and Harvesting the Sea

Jason Whooley

Jason Whooley is the CEO of Bio-marine Ingredients Ireland (BII), formerly head of Bord Iascaigh Mhara and before that the South and West Fishermen's Organisation in Castletownbere. The essay below is from a Thomas Davis Lecture broadcast on Seascapes on RTÉ Radio 1 in 2002.

When I began as Manager of the Irish South & West Fishermen's Organisation I had just finished college. I was approaching the job as an ordinary member of the public. I knew very little about the profession, very little about the Industry or its people. I suppose I had a romantic notion about fishing as a way of life – fishermen in their oilskins, heading out to sea and returning laden down with fish.

I have had the benefit of six years' exposure to the industry which has allowed me reform my views about the profession. Even after a few weeks my views had changed. Things weren't as they appeared. A fisherman's job is tough, this industry is tough. There is very little romantic about it. Unlike people involved in the Industry the general public don't fully comprehend what's involved, unfortunately neither do the politicians of this country.

It is my belief that this lack of understanding has been one of the biggest obstacles to the industry down through the years and continues to be a major impediment to the necessary development of the fishing industry. When explaining our needs to the general public we as representatives often find ourselves using farming analogies to describe out circumstances. Unlike farming, very few people have had exposure to the fishing industry. Practically everyone in Ireland has been on a farm or knows someone who has a farm or their relations came from a farming community. It means there is an awareness of the farming needs. It means that the general public can empathise with a farmer when he states his case. It's completely different with fishing. There is no real level of understanding. Maybe it is a failure of the industry to convey their messages but it is this lack of-understanding which is really our main hindrance as a fishing country.

This lack of understanding means we don't realise the potential of our coastal waters. We could have a massive Industry worth hundreds of millions of Euros each year to the country. It would create vast employment in coastal areas where there are few economic alternatives. During the World Cup there was a beer advert doing the rounds and it could be applied to the fishing industry. It would go something like this: Ireland doesn't realise it has a fishing industry, but if it did it would probably be the best in the world.

Our lack of understanding of our industry isn't a recent phenomenon; it's been there for hundreds of years: in 1550, 600 Spanish boats were said to be fishing off the southwest coast. We have never been fully aware of the abundance of fish in our waters. Even with other nations pointing us in the right direction the penny still hadn't dropped, we still don't appreciate the full potential of our fishing industry. Never was this more evident than when we joined the EU. We negotiated a lamentable deal. Some would say we traded agriculture for fishing. Others say we didn't realise what we were doing; other opinions state we were poor negotiators. Whatever the deal the result remains unchanged.

The foundations for the Common Fisheries Policy (CFP) were laid in 1970 when the original six Member States signed the CFP and introduced what is called 'Equal Access' principle, which allows all countries access to what is a common resource. That principal was the key issue for the entry of the four applicant countries of that time: Norway, Denmark, UK and Ireland. Even though Norway signed the Treaty of Accession, their Fisheries Minister resigned and the Norwegian people voted No to joining the EEC. We joined with 16% of EU waters yet we were only allocated 4% of quotas. This deal set the scene for the Irish fishing industry in EU fishing policy. It means that we constantly face an uphill battle in quota terms making significant progress or development in the industry more difficult.

We can only look with envy at our new neighbours who have vast quantities of quotas. For example, our French counterparts have annual surplus of quotas which they cannot catch. In some instances these surpluses exceed the total quota which is allocated to Ireland. I am sure you will agree a farcical situation but unfortunately a very real one for the Irish Fishing Industry. It's very unpalatable for the Industry, very difficult for them to operate with and to comprehend but it is a very real part of their everyday existence. Controls, regulations and bureaucracy most of which emanates from Brussels make a fisherman's job even tougher.

What is a fisherman's life really like? Imagine going to sea for seven or maybe even ten days and not returning home, living in a confined space with six, seven or eight others. This lifestyle was brought home to me one night when I came down from Dublin by train and one of our vessels was tied to the quay in Cork. I went on board for a cup of coffee before continuing on my journey to Castletownbere. I was absolutely amazed by the small area in which these guys had to live in on a weekly basis. I had the comfort of being able to get off and sit into my car, go home and spend the night in bed. For these men it was another week out fishing, very little romantic about it.

It's a fact of life – these vessels have to work. They are small businesses involving huge amounts of capital. The vessel is a fixed asset without it' there is no income so it has to keep working. Nowadays with even greater levels of capital involved vessels spend more time at sea. They turn around after unloading their catch and are back out on the fishing grounds inside twenty-four hours. It's become a very serious business operation. Some of the vessels will now work ten-day trips, with crew's doing two ten-day trips and then having ten days off. The operation continues through weekends, bad weather, etc. but it's what is needed to compete with other fishing nations.

Before the advent of the 'Celtic Tiger' crews for the industry were not a major difficulty, however with plenty of onshore alternatives, particularly in the building sector, crews have become more and more difficult to attract and retrain. It has meant looking elsewhere for crewmen – Eastern Europe has become more popular. There we can source trained crewmen who are redundant following the withdrawal of the Russian factory ships. Without them and crews from other countries some of our vessels wouldn't be going to sea. They have become an everyday part of the fishing industry, part and parcel of a growing economy. In traditional sectors like this there will always be labour shortages, fishing is one of those sectors. Crew are an integral part of our industry, essential to the working of the business.

From the late 1970s onwards the industry effectively went backwards when compared with our EU neighbours. Far too often our policymakers adopted a cautious approach, we dipped our toe while others dived straight in. As a country we were like penguins shuffling along the ice, waiting for someone else to he-move. As a result we are playing catch-up and it is a very difficult race to catch up in. Recently, thanks to the BIM Whitefish Development Programme, we have been able to renew our older vessels; prior to that we had the second oldest fleet in Europe. For over twenty years there were no new buildings in Ireland in the whitefish industry. Had we had the political will, the understanding, the foresight we would be serious players in EU fishing terms. Twenty years later the BIM Programme clearly showed what could be done, consistent landings, good working conditions for crew and low maintenance costs. It acted as a catalyst, it had a vision with funding to match. It brought confidence to everyone in the industry. This vision or strategy had been completely lacking in our industry for too long. We were reactive, never proactive.

As I mentioned, the new boats have encouraged other owners to modernise which has brought a consistency of fish landings that can't be under estimated. If there is bad weather then the boats won't be fishing, the crew won't be happy, customers won't be happy. No one in coastal areas will be happy. This is something that is lost on the ordinary public. coastal communities depend almost completely on fishing. The boats are like small factories or large households. Weekly grocery bills can be enormous, a major boost to local shopkeepers and local butchers. When they are fishing there is money in the community, when they are not everybody has problems. Fishing is the lifeblood of these communities.

These last few months everyone knows how bad the weather has been. How many weeks have we had incessant rain? It is not the rain that bothers fishermen, it is wind, gales and storms. The rain has bothered Joe Public, the weather has been bad, but has it meant that he has had no wages for the past three months? That's what it means to the fishing industry and to their families. If we were farmers the fishermen keep saying to me we would get compensated but there is none of that for the fishing industry. Compensation is against the rules of the Common Fisheries Policy – it's difficult to swallow especially when you see your rural neighbours being treated differently. Last year £1.4 billion came from Brussels for farmers. Why are we different? Could we learn from the farmers? Fishermen say, the IFA will help us. What people don't realise is that the IFA have 80,000 members and 949 branches. That's a massive organisation with huge political clout. I think we have to get real. Farming is a political priority in this country and that's why results are delivered.

Fishermen are treated differently not just to farmers but to other seafarers. In recent budgets seafarers who travel on merchant ships were given a seafarers' allowance in recognition of their difficult jobs. Some of these seafarers may spend only four hours on a channel crossing and yet they get €6,000 in additional tax-free allowance, yet our fishermen who spend ten days at sea are entitled to nothing. It's unsatisfactory, but this industry and its people are nothing if not resilient. In recent years progress has been made; we have been moving forward.

Unfortunately, last month, with one stroke from the Government, the industry was dealt a hammer blow. After the election, the Taoiseach saw fit to effectively do away with the Department of the Marine – even the title 'Marine' was dropped from the new amalgamated Department of Communications and Natural Resources. As you can appreciate, it resulted in total out-cry from the industry. 'Marine' is now back in the title but a dedicated Marine Department is effectively gone. This is a major blow for the industry. It signals a real lack of interest or understanding on the Government's behalf. Do they not realise we have a fishing industry? Do they not realise we are a fishing nation, an island surrounded by water? As one of my fishermen said, 'it seems every other country wants our fish except us'. It makes you wonder. Think back to 1550: 600 foreign vessels off the southwest coast. Have we lost the plot?

These fishermen from other countries want our fish and they want it badly obviously, quite an amount more than our Government. Foreign fleets comprising of state of the art vessels are a regular feature off our south and west coasts. New vessels, quite obviously heavily supported by their Governments, now effectively base themselves in our southwestern ports just landing their catches into the back of trucks for transport to French and Spanish markets. This is one of the most difficult pills for the industry to swallow. Why is it that these seem to get so much support and us so little? I believe it would have been politically suicidal to demote the Department of Fisheries in Spain or France. These countries have a tradition in fishing, they realised 500 years ago what this renewable resource could yield. Why don't we plan for the future? There is a future, we must stop looking at today and plan ahead for five, ten and fifteen years' time.

Perhaps people think they'll be no fish left in five years' time. There is no question that there isn't as much fish in the sea as there used to be. If you believe some of the press you'd think that there is nothing left out there. This is completely untrue. It's a dramatic story, probably the one that mostly frequents the media from a fishing viewpoint, that and our December Council of Ministers Meeting which sets the TACs for the coming year. Both stories convey the same message: fish stocks are gone, no more cod and chips. The message is simple, easy to understand and generally taken on board by the public. Unfortunately, it creates an image for politicians and public alike, an image that is difficult to change. What young person will commit their future to an industry on this basis, what bank will invest given these stories? This is where the industry needs to educate. Take two stocks recently identified by the EU scientists to be in crisis: cod and hake. Last year both had recovery plans introduced; EU fishermen had argued against these saying the science was inaccurate. Subsequently, scientists have reversed their decision for hake and it's now off the agenda.

In the case of cod it is a similar story. Off the southwest English coast this spring there was so much cod that fishermen's organisations banned their fishermen from catching it. It couldn't be sold, the price collapsed. Is this a indicator of a stock on the verge of collapse, on the verge of extinction? At the same time, we have certain Green lobbyists encouraging consumers to switch to alternative foods to save the fish. One experienced fisherman said to me years ago, 'fish have an awful tendency to make fools of us', and I think he is right. Yes, stocks aren't where they were twenty years ago but they are not on the verge of extinction. There are problems but are they due to over-fishing? I think not. This year pilchards were seen in huge quantities off the southwest coast, which hasn't been the case for twenty years. Pilchards were the mainstay of the southwestern fleet 400 years ago. Tuna has become more commonplace off the southwest coast during summer months, anchovies are appearing in the northwest. All of these factors point to a changing environment. Who knows what effect this changing environment is having on our traditional stocks? We don't know, the scientists don't know and certainly the European Commission doesn't know. The Commission's response to this uncertainty is to blame it on over-fishing – just cut the quotas, cut the fishermen, fishermen are expendable.

This is the EU mentality; it is simple and blunt. Simple and blunt it may be but it is the only way bureaucrats in Brussels have of dealing with the problem. They can't manage real solutions. They are dealing with migratory fish stocks that don't follow rules and regulations. Can you imagine what will be done when another ten countries join the political negotiations? I shudder to think. Quota and fleet cuts have not worked since the introduction of the Common Fisheries Policy and they won't work in the future.

Fishermen aren't really involved in this EU decision making. The officials in Brussels, regardless of the views from the industry, will go their own way. In a democracy, we as an industry should be involved but we are not; we should be contributing to policy making but we are not.

As I mentioned earlier, our poor experience with Brussels began with our very entry. Our recent track record in that period hasn't been much better. It's no one's fault – we have three votes out of 84 in Brussels. One more than Luxembourg and the same as Austria and we all know what massive fishing nations they are. The bottom line is that we don't get anything at Brussels unless somebody else wants it also. The Common Fisheries Policy, which supposedly leg-islates the fishing industry, is an embarrassment. Its negotiations are nothing short of shambolic and there isn't a shred of logic to the ma-jority to the EU Commission's fishery actions. Take the recent Deep Water quota allocations. Scientific advice was that quotas were not the way forward for these species yet the proposals were accepted. Where's the logic, where's the conservation policy? It's a political game, a game which unfortunately has severe repercussions for those depending on it for a living.

In the fishing industry we have countless examples of how Brus-sels has operated in this fashion. The Irish tuna driftnetting fishery is a perfect example. Irish fishermen got involved in this fishery and made a success of it. This was unacceptable to some of our European partners, Green lobbyists got involved and driftnetting banned. It was all done in the absence of scientific advice.

Part of the Common Fisheries Policy is the Hague Preferences which guarantees Ireland a certain amount of fishing quotas. Dur-ing the negotiations last December in Brussels the Commission at-tempted to take those entitlements from us. Had our Minister and officials not put up an excellent fight we would have lost these enti-tlements. This is the type of environment we exist in – not a democ-racy at all. Those talks at Christmas are a classic example of how the Commission and how the fisheries policy work. Thirty- seven hours of constant negotiations, no sleep, a battle of wills deciding on the quotas for the coming months. It's good TV, makes good headlines. The question must be asked, is this how we should deal with people's livelihoods? Should we have a better system in operation? Depriv-ing people of sleep and expecting them to make rational decisions, surely that can't be achieved under this kind of regime. The public and media are all interested for one night but the fishing industry has to live with those decisions for 364 nights.

At the end of this year we have the Common Fisheries Policy review and judging on what I have outlined I am obviously not altogether optimistic that we will get the results we need. We need significant results, we need coastal protection for our fishermen and we need a fair share of quotas. These are realistic expectations but in the politically-driven climate which is Brussels I am not optimistic. It's a major source of concern for the fishing industry. We feel at times we are banging our heads off a brick wall. It's interesting that the vote on Nice is back on the agenda. From my viewpoint the European approach has to change. If any other industry was getting the same treatment as the fishermen at Brussels the answer to Nice would be a resounding No.

What about the future of the fishing industry? Without question, the CFP negotiations are absolutely crucial. We need a better deal, we need at least maintenance of the existing regulations covering the Irish Box. These regulations limit access to Irish coastal waters for the Spanish fleet to a certain number at any one time, we need this to continue. We need to ensure that our stocks are adequately protected and policed. From a fleet point of view we have only 2.5 per cent of the European Union fleet and we can't tolerate any fleet reductions.

Rationalisation has taken place in our industry and will continue to happen. It's undesirable but like most industries it is inevitable. Take a look at our farming neighbours again; the same thing has happened and will continue to happen with fishing. Despite the inevitable wastage, we still need to develop a modern and efficient fleet capable of catching a diverse range of species, capable of opening new opportunities for themselves. This may be achieved by amalgamating vessels, creating more partnerships. I must stress these vessels are highly capitalised assets, they cannot be tied up for long periods.

With a developed fleet I am sure this industry has a very bright future. It can develop and it should develop but it is going to take commitment from our Government at the highest level to ensure that this development takes place. Senior politicians must take an interest; it's too easy to shrug the shoulders and find an excuse. As I said already, recent events would lead you to believe that there is an absence of the necessary commitment. Throwing money when times are good at an industry will not suffice if it we are to have a long-term future.

Today in Ireland it appears that everything needs to have a Balance Sheet and Profit and Loss statement. It's an unfortunate consequence of the 'Celtic Tiger'. We tend to judge things solely on a financial basis. Take a look at the bottom line, does it add up? Is it making a profit? It's a bit like our bus routes or the Post Offices – if they are not making a profit then there is an argument for scrapping them. Rural Ireland can't be judged like that. Included in that is the fishing industry. It is essential to our social fabric. We need to keep these people in the coastal areas. We need to maintain their way of living otherwise people will converge on urban centres and increase or multiply our existing urban problems like housing and traffic. If we are not careful, areas will become little more than villages of holiday homes.

- We need a coherent strategy for the future. We must decide where we want this industry to go and have a roadmap on how to get there. This needs to be based largely on what the leading countries are doing.

- We need our Government's total commitment. Lip service for the industry isn't good enough – real commitments with real plans and budgets are needed. We only expect and deserve the same as other sectors of the economy.

- We must innovate – forget about looking backwards. What has been done in the past will not work in the future. Let's develop a coherent policy, let's create the environment that will support our entrepreneurs in the sector. If we do then I'm convinced we can build a hugely successful fishing industry.

Remember, Ireland doesn't realise it has a fishing industry, but if it did . . .

Roche's Point

10

Ireland's Lighthouses

John Eagle

An extract from Ireland's Lighthouses – A Photo Essay by John Eagle

Roche's Point

Nearest place: Whitegate
Location: Lat/Long: 51º 47' 06" N, 8º 15' 03" W
OSI 'Discovery' Series: 81/87
Situation: Mainland

How to get there: This lighthouse is accessible but it is easy to miss the right turning. Drive east from Cork city, following signs to Waterford, until you reach Midleton. Turn off and follow signs to Whitegate. From Whitegate, keep on the main road. There is a turn off to the right rising steeply to a large industrial complex: do not turn up this road, instead take the next right-hand turn. Follow to the end and over the crest of a hill the lighthouse will come into view.

Lighthouse details

Built: 1835
Structure: White tower
Elevation: 30 m

Range: W 20 nm; R 16 nm

Character: Oc WR 20s

Sited on the north-side entrance to Cork Harbour. The original tower of 1817 was dismantled and taken to Duncannon, as it was deemed too small for Cork Harbour. The present 15-metre-high tower was built in 1835. It stands 30 metres above sea level.

It was by pure chance that I captured the late lamented Irish sail-training vessel *Asgard II* in one of these pictures. I had met a friend for a cup of tea in Cronins in Crosshaven that day, not meaning to stay long. However, one word borrowed another and several hours passed before we went up to Weaver's Point to get the photos, with sunset not far off. Had I gone up at the time originally planned, we would have missed the wonderful sight of *Asgard II* sailing in. My thanks to Captain Brendan Creedon of Gaelic Helicopters for flying me.

Straw Island

Straw Island

Nearest place: Kilronan
Location: Lat/Long: 53° 7' 0" N, 9° 37' 9" W
OSI 'Discovery' Series: 51
Situation: On an offshore island

How to get there: This lighthouse can be seen from the regular passenger ferries that travel between the Aran Islands and the mainland (they leave for Inishmore from Rossaveel and Galway, and Doolin in County Clare). Landing on the island might not be easy. To get to Rossaveel take the R336 west from Galway town. Ask at the pier if there is a local boat owner who would be willing to take you out there.

Lighthouse details

Built: 1 September 1878
Structure: White tower
Elevation: 11 m
Range: 15 nm
Character: Fl (2) W 5s
De-manned: 30 September 1926

Sited on an island off the east coast of Inishmore this lighthouse was established on 1 September 1878. It was converted to unwatched with an acetylene light on 30 September 1926 and electrified on 23 August 1980 using a wind generator to charge the batteries.

Hook Head

Nearest place: Fethard
Location: Lat/Long: 52° 07' 03" N, 6° 55' 07" W
OSI 'Discovery' Series: 76
Situation: Mainland, public access

Hook Head

How to get there: From Waterford go to the Passage East Ferry, then on the Wexford side of the river follow signs for Hook Head. From Wexford follow signs to Passage East Ferry, looking out for signs to Hook Head pointing to your left. The lighthouse is open to the public, guided tours are given up the tower and there is also a gift shop and cafeteria there. A nice day out for the family.

Lighthouse details
Built: c. 1172
Structure: White tower, two black bands
Elevation: 46 m
Range: 23 nm

Character: Fl W 3s

De-manned: 29 March 1996

Established c. 1172, Hook Head is one of the oldest lighthouses in Europe, and was originally looked after by monks. The present optic was installed in 1910. The light was electrified from 1 August 1972 and automated from 29 March 1996. It has a range of 23 nautical miles.

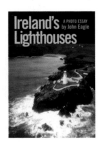

From *Ireland's Lighthouses – A Photo Essay* by John Eagle, published by The Collins Press, www.collins-press.ie

Celebrating Seascape's 1,000th edition in December 2008 – Marcus Connaughton,
Kevin Healy, Kevin Fowley, Michael McLoughlin, Tom MacSweeney
(photo by Margaret Brown)

Marcus and Tom confer over a programme change at the 1,000th edition
of Seascapes (photo by Margaret Brown)

11

John de Courcy Ireland

Hugh Oram

Hugh Oram is a Dublin-based writer and broadcaster, who has contributed to RTÉ Radio 1 for over 30 years, including Seascapes since its earliest days. He has also contributed for a similar period to The Irish Times, as well as to many other print and online publications in Ireland and internationally.

One of the greatest figures in Irish maritime history, Dr John de Courcy Ireland, died eight years ago on 4 April 2006. Memories of him and of all the work he did to promote the Irish maritime tradition live on strongly. He was a wonderful person and I was one of many people with an interest in maritime matters who was privileged to have known him.

The first time I met him was at his modest home in Dalkey, and once he had got started on his reminiscences and his anecdotes about the sea, there was no stopping him. His skills at storytelling helped him become a firm favourite on *Seascapes* over many years.

On one occasion, he had enthused about how when you emerge from the railway station in Marseilles, and stand at the top of the great flight of steps that leads to the city below, you will be enthused by the tremendous view over the port of Marseilles. A short time after that, I happened to arrive in Marseilles by train and found the view exactly as he had described it with such enthusiasm.

He was born in Lucknow in India in 1911, the son of a County Kildare man who was serving in the British Army. His father died from a fever a short while later and John was eventually sent home to go to school at Marlborough College in England. He recalled later that his stepfather was a ghastly man and that as a diversion, he started reading the Encyclopedia Brittanica from cover to cover.

His adventures at sea began when he was 17 and he ran away to serve as a deckhand on a Dutch freighter sailing to South America. It was a fine introduction to the maritime world, but he came back and went up to Oxford. It was there that he met Beatrice Haigh, usually called Betty, who was working in a café there. They married when they were both 21 and went on to have one son and two daughters. In typical John de Courcy Ireland style, the first thing they did after they were married was to spend some months living on the Aran Islands and in County Donegal to improve their Irish. John was nothing if not a perfectionist.

His wife became a nurse in Barcelona during the Spanish civil war. An early indication of John's political views came in 1940, when he was 29 years of age and working in a ship's chandlers in Derry. He found himself sacked because of all his trade union activity.

Eventually, he completed his education at Trinity College in Dublin, where he got his PhD in 1951 for his dissertation on the influence of the sea on civilisation. He always used to say that the sea bound people together.

John made a lifelong career out of teaching, first at St Patrick's Cathedral Grammar School in Dublin, then at Drogheda Grammar School, going on to Bandon Grammar School in County Cork. In 1968, he joined the staff of Kingstown Grammar School in Dun Laoire. It eventually became Newpark Comprehensive. John stayed there until 1986, which meant that he had carried on as a teacher until he was 75.

In 1943, he was a founder of the Maritime Institute of Ireland and remained on its council for 55 years, as well as being its research officer. In 1959, he was one those instrumental in setting up the Maritime Museum in Dun Laoire. In that harbour town, too, he was secretary of the local lifeboat for over 25 years; he was also a life governor of the RNLI.

He wrote some very learned books on maritime history and his last book, in 2001, was a history of Dun Laoire harbour. Out of the plaques erected in his honour, the one that pleased him most was that in the People's Park in Dun Laoire, because it was the only one that mentioned his wife, Betty, who died in 1999.

John received honours and recognition from many countries around the world, from Argentina to China, France to the old Yugoslavia. He was simply unstoppable, and on his 90th birthday he was to be found in Melilla, one of the two Spanish enclaves on the northern coast of Morocco. It was in Melilla that the world's first lifeboat service had been organised and John, naturally, wanted to find out more.

Apart from all his maritime interests, he was keenly involved in such organisations as the Irish Anti-Apartheid Movement and the Irish Campaign for Nuclear Disarmament; John was a lifelong pacifist. He and his wife Betty were always committed to left-wing causes and, deep down, his two passions, apart from his wife, were humanity and the sea. A remarkably knowledgeable but modest man, people couldn't help but find him endearing, no matter what their own political views.

We remember him as the great crusader for the Irish maritime and marine sector and indeed for the sailing confraternity the world over.

Dunbrody in dry dock in New Ross boatyard (photo by Marcus Connaughton)

12

Pulling Together: Irish Seafarers and Trade Union Organisation

Francis Devine

Francis Devine is a retired trade union official and author of Organising History: A Centenary of SIPTU, 1909-2009. He is an honorary president of the Irish Labour History Society and former editor of Saothar. The essay below is from one of the six Thomas Davis Lectures that aired on Seascapes.

L ittle has been written about the organisation of Irish seafarers. What follows is a tentative sketch. It suggests a colourful history of international solidarity, constant battles against employer scandal and Government indifference and a deep commitment, beyond self-interest, to the development of an Irish merchant marine. I offer the lecture to the memory of the late Bernard Malone – Barney to his Irish Shipping comrades and Benny in his native Howth where he was much loved.

Early Attempts at Organising Seamen
Organisation among seamen existed from the 1840s from Derry to Cork, Belfast to ·Wexford. The 'friendly society' aspect dominated and seamen and masters often combined in the same organisation for sick, burial and benevolent purposes. Fishermen were

organised in Ringsend and Cork Harbour, the Fishermen's Society of Saint Patrick banner being among those that paraded in the 1875 O'Connell Centenary. The 1873 banner of the Boyne Fishermen, which hangs in Drogheda's Millmount Musuem, is a 'masterpiece, painted in oils on canvas and worthy of exhibition in any gallery in the world'. As with Shannon eel fishers today, concerns were for licences, access and quotas rather than wages and conditions. Fishermen have sporadically organised since. The Irish Transport & General Workers' Union recruited large numbers in the mid-1970s, the legacy of a long-gone organisation being that fishermen, uniquely among Irish seafarers, are covered within the terms of the Unfair Dismissals Act, 1977-2001, a rare extension of protective employment law to the sea.

The Merchant Shipping Acts reinforced command structures and what might be an industrial dispute ashore could be mutiny at sea. In addition, Irish mariners tended to ship out of their home ports where relationships with owners and masters were close and the cost of failed trade union activity was ostracism and/or emigration. Many, of course, always sought work on British lines and it was here, in 1887, that Joseph Havelock Wilson established the National Amalgamated Sailors' & Firemen's Union of Great Britain. Branches were opened in Arklow, Cork, Wexford and Youghal. In 1890, a three month dockers' strike in support of sacked Cork seamen spread to Waterford and Limerick as employers attacked the infant union. Shipowners resented the 'tyrannical attempts of a dictatorial body of unionists to impose demands on the industry', and in September, 1890, the Shipping Federation emerged as a powerful employer body, supplying strike breakers and influencing mercantile law.

Until the 1890s, trade unionism had been confined to the traditional skilled trades and was conservative politically and industrially. The so-called 'New Unionism' that now exploded on to the waterfront extended organisation down to the unskilled masses, involved sympathetic and general strikes and carried a distinctly socialist perspective. Often seen as originating among dock workers, 'New Unionism' more correctly can be attributed to seamen. In 1894, Wilson revived his union as the National Sailors' & Firemen's Union of Great Britain & Ireland. By 1896 branches existed in Belfast, Cork and Dublin. They were difficult to maintain, however, and in 1898 Irish offices were closed with staff owed monies. At this point Wilson was still 'militant, a rabble-rouser, a fearless advocate of the seafarer, stumping the country agitating, organizing and inciting'. He was the Jim Larkin of seamen and in 1911 came his finest hour.

1911, Wilson's Finest Hour – 1913, Wilson's Disgrace

By April, over 150,000 seamen had voted for international action 'on the same day and at the same hour, until their unions receive proper recognition, establish the right of collective bargaining and uniform rates of wages and conditions of labour on all ships'. Similar international strike action would be relevant today in the struggle against Flags of Convenience and the slave wages paid to seamen across the globe. In 1911 what followed broke the Shipping Federation's power and won a general increase in wages. Wilson's triumph contained the seeds of his rapid shift to the right as he sought strategies that would preserve his gains, keep control of the 'ticket' from the Shipping Federation and maintain the advantage of newly-acquired respectability.

Irish seamen fought hard in 1911. Dublin flags proclaimed 'War Is Now Declared: Seamen Strike Hard & Strike For Liberty'. It was, however, Big Jim Larkin's Transport Union – appointed as agents by the Sailors & Firemen – that represented the 400 Dublin members and paid them strike pay from Transport Union funds. The desire to assist seamen in Belfast led to James Connolly's appointment as Northern Organiser on 13 July 1911, Connolly's first full-time union position.

Irish employers, led by Samuel McCormick, refused to concede and 800 men were locked out until Larkin and the celebrated British labour veteran, Tom Mann, met with the Under Secretary for Ireland, and persuaded the employers to accept the union's terms. In January, 1913, there were strikes on the City of Dublin Steam Packet

Company and in Sligo, the Transport Union again representing seamen. As the 1913 lock out reached stalemate, Havelock Wilson, as a member of the Trades Union Congress Parliamentary Committee, appeared as 'reason personified' in appreciating the employer's perspective and suggesting conciliation. Wilson despised Larkin, to whom Dublin seamen were more loyal. Wilson suggested Larkin 'had a splendid case but made such a sorry mess of it, doing everything he ought not to have done and nothing he ought'. Larkin responded with vituperation and Wilson's decision to settle with the employers caused outrage. Dublin sailors refused to go back and were quickly replaced by Sailors' & Firemen's Union members from Liverpool. Even the heroic steamship *Hare* that had nobly brought in the first food shipment for the lock out victims was declared a 'blackleg boat'. Connolly witheringly suggested that 'the scab who carries a union card is the scabbiest of all scabs'. Dublin seamen would be slow to forgive the Sailors' Union.

It is seldom considered that 1913 was essentially a maritime dispute. As now, the economy depended on trade through Dublin. Connolly tried to close the port 'as tight as a drum' in a desperate effort to break the deadlock as indication of his appreciation of the strategic significance of the sea. The food ships' attempts to ship out the many starving children, the dependence of so many workers and their families on the maritime economy all underline the neglected fact that the sea was the central issue in 1913. The fact that this is never acknowledged is part of the mental block that denies the country's maritime dependence.

The Birth of Irish Seamen's Unions

After 1913, the Transport Union represented seamen and fought a wage reduction of six shillings and sixpence imposed by the British Maritime Board in 1923 in Belfast, Cork, Dublin, Dundalk, Limerick, Newry and Waterford. The compliance of the Sailors' & Firemen's Union made the Transport Union task very difficult and they failed to break the Maritime Board's control of Irish seamen's wages. Seamen on the B&I struck unofficially the same year to protest over discrimination in crew selection and to demand the reinstatement of the wage cut. It began a rift between seamen and the Transport Union, whose docker members always bore the brunt of seamen's struggles.

In 1926, the Sailors' & Firemen's Union changed its name to the National Union of Seamen. In Dublin, in 1933, the Irish Seamen & Port Workers' Union was founded, followed by the Irish Free State Pilots' Association in 1935. Boosted by membership in Irish shipping, the Irish Seamen & Portworkers campaigned for the establishment of an Irish Maritime Board. They had won 'out-of-convoy' bonuses during the war to demonstrate the value of being able to negotiate directly with employers. An Irish Maritime Board was set up on 15 October, 1948. The British Maritime Board's objectives were to secure 'closer co-operation between the employers and employed of the British Mercantile Marine in the maintenance of the supremacy of the British Empire', objectives surely at odds with the strategic needs of the Irish nation or its seafarers? Opposition to the NUS was not merely a nationalistic expression but reflected tensions over crewing methods.

In 1951, the Irish Seamen & Port Workers had a signal victory in a wage claim, having rejected an initial Labour Court recommendation. The principle involved in this dispute was that an Irish union successfully negotiated wages and conditions for Irish seamen, separate and distinct from British seamen. Seamen were becoming a force in the Irish Seamen & Port Workers, and in 1954 Des Branigan emerged as a new, intelligently focused and charismatic advocate. The union changed its name in 1955 to the Marine, Port & General Workers' Union. Branigan's legacy includes the wonderful badge that bears the silver starry plough and triple knot of Saint Brendan the Navigator against a deep blue background. The starry ensign represents Irish socialism and the navigational safety of members at sea, and the knot's Celtic interweave exemplifies the interdependence and solidarity essential to trade union members. At Congress of Irish Union gatherings, Branigan led demands for the proper development of Irish shipping. The country possessed less than half the minimum recommended tonnage of 250,000 tons and no tanker fleet. Norway was cited as example of a successful maritime policy that not alone underlined the country's neutrality and independence but contributed significantly to the balance of payments.

Branigan's radical militancy offended powerful clerical figures and moves were made to oust him from the Marine Port, the chosen vehicle being the jettisoning of the union's seamen's section. In 1957, a closed shop agreement – always denied to Branigan – was offered to a new body, the Irish Seamen's Union. This new union was seen by many as a company union and was opposed in rancorous and unseemly dispute. Ship owners in Limerick and Wexford threatened to sail under the British flag in order to deal with the NUS, and employers generally openly stated their desire to stamp out what they called an undesirable element which was controlling Dublin port. After a 14-week strike, matters were resolved by the Labour Court and in 1959 the Seamen's Union of Ireland emerged as an independent union acceptable to the men.

Des Branigan was now General Secretary of the Irish Pilots' & Marine Officers' Association and he set about seeking reform of the Pilotage Act, 1913 that condemned pilots to meagre earnings from casual work. Less than a hundred in number, Branigan pointed out that it was 'through the hands and skill of the marine pilots that the country's imports and exports arrive and depart safely'. A bitter dispute was defeated and the broken union merged with the Workers' Union of Ireland in 1962. Branigan still pushed for a maritime policy, telling the Irish Trade Union Congress that 'we have the geographical advantage, we have the trained personnel, we have every advantage if we want to exploit them'. He concluded that 'it lies with the Government if this desirable advance is to take place'.

The Battle to Win the NUS for Seamen

The NUS were a silent delegation to Irish TUCs. They were still recovering from their ostracism after the 1926 General Strike and

Wilson's pursuit of 'non-political trade unionism'. Wilson died at his desk on 16 April 1929. King George V and Queen Mary sent a letter of sympathy to Mrs Wilson. Lord Sanderson, Shipping Federation, observed that he was a 'dictator in the affairs of the seamen' and 'one of the few really constructive thinkers in the trade union movement'. *The Miner* spoke for the majority and reflected the attitude to Wilson within the British labour movement even to this day:

> *We do not propose to overstep the bounds of good taste in our comments on Havelock Wilson.... The War had a most disturbing effect upon his outlook and in post war years he has been, in plain language, a faithful ally of the employing class. His union ... has been a faithful servant of the ship-owners and he himself used the whole of his own and his union's influence to disrupt and demoralise other sections.... He will go down in history as one of the tragedies of the twentieth century working class movement.*

Wilson's legacy, compounded by the economic collapse of the 1930s, was a highly centralised and rigid union structure. Seamen had no trade union presence while at sea. The Merchant Shipping Act, 1894, made no provision for shipboard representation and enshrined absolute authority in the lawful command of the master. The command culture permeated the NUS where the General Secretary was the all-powerful captain of a trade union ironclad.

Mutiny slowly boiled and in 1960 the National Seamen's Reform Movement set about the task of winning the union back for ordinary seamen. Waterford-born Paddy Neary was a leading figure and Dungarvan's Sean Cullinane typical of the many rank-and-file Irish seamen who joined the reformers. General Secretary Sir Tom Yates branded them as 'communists dedicated to disruption' and 'self-styled militants whose minds are so closed that the whole development of collective bargaining has passed them by'. A strike in 1960 advanced wages and conditions and shipboard representation was finally agreed in 1965.

In 1966 a strike on the principle of the 40-hour week comparable to shore workers lasted seven weeks and by 1 July saw 891 ships immobilised. Prime Minister Harold Wilson declared a State of Emergency and talked of a 'tightly knit group of politically motivated men'. The NUS was isolated nationally and internationally.

Some saw the strike as disaster, others saw it as the union 'coming of age'. Above all, it at last cast aside the image of an Uncle Tom organisation dominated and manipulated by the ship owners. The ghost of the collaborationist Havelock Wilson was laid to rest.

Two thousand people – 500 of them seamen – marched in Belfast on 21 May and Irish solidarity generally was impressive. Gerry Doyle reflected on the strike in a letter attacking Harold Wilson and George Brown, suggesting that 'the cost to the country compared to the cost of meeting the seamen's claim is proof that this Government is quite willing to cut its throat to cure laryngitis'. Irish support saw the NUS affiliate to the ICTU and Belfast Trades Council. The 1967 NUS AGM was held in Liberty Hall as a gesture of gratitude to the Irish labour movement and Irish people for their support in adversity.

Terry Clare, steward on the Rosslare–Fishguard line, was elected to the NUS Executive Committee in 1955 and held that position until retirement in 1991. He took his Executive duties very seriously but worked hard 'to get this union to swing a little more to the left'. When Sir Thomas Yates retired as General Secretary, he singled out Clare as 'someone who never agreed with me'. Clare was a founder of the Merchant Navy ratings Pension Fund. His pension interest was dismissed by leftist seamen as indication of his middle class orientation but this was a short-sighted view. The collapse of the fund was a bitter blow to Clare, now active in the Pensioner's Parliament and a vigorous campaigner for the aged at national and local levels. He was awarded the British Empire Medal in 1982 in recognition of his pensions activity. He never missed an Executive meeting.

Barney Crossan, a Glen Swilly man, had many years deep-water experience before gaining a reputation as a NUS Official in the

Thames Basin. He became Dublin Branch Secretary in 1963 and, when he retired in 1991, not one of his members was out of work. A quietly effective figure, Crossan's social conscience endeared him to all seamen and generated commitment from shore-based trade union colleagues when a ship needed to be listed or a cargo blacked. Nothing was either too much trouble or too late at a night, whether the seaman was a NUS member or not. Dublin Branch regularly contributed to national union affairs, tending to concentrate on bread-and-butter issues of annual leave, pay and conditions.

After the fruitless dispute with P&O in Dover in 1988, the NUS's fate as an independent union with a declining membership and perilous finances was sealed. They merged with the National Union of Railwaymen in 1991 to form the National Union of Rail, Maritime & Transport Workers. Seamen were soon swamped by the rail sections and rule changes quickly obliterated most traces of a once proud union.

The Scandal of Irish Shipping and Sales of the Century

Seamen on the Irish Sea negotiated various Container and General Purpose Agreements in the 1960s and 1970s. The Seamen's Union of Ireland once picketed RTÉ in defence of their members employed by the national broadcaster as riggers! In 1984 the Government liquidated Irish Shipping. There were fears for Irish Continental Line, Belfast Car Ferries and the B&I. Speaking against the closure of Irish Shipping, Terry Clare said that the 'Dáil and the nation were held in contempt'. Justice Murphy had found that there was no fraud involved but Clare said, 'What rubbish, fraud was perpetrated on the people of Ireland and the seafarers of Ireland'. Anger was unbounded. The Federated Workers' Union of Ireland mounted a ceaseless campaign, picketing the Dáil, Ministers' homes and anywhere that the 'Save Our Ships' campaign could attract support, as well as making endless appearances before the Labour Court and Employment Appeals tribunal in defence of the sacked members' interests.

Taosieach Garret FitzGerald's memory of the affair shows some unease and it was 'one of the most painful decisions we had to take while in Government'. Ordinary Irish Shipping staff were the only sacrificed state sector employees in this period of severe retrenchment to be confined to statutory redundancy payments. The subsequent response to the Insurance Corporation of Ireland-Allied Irish Banks scandal makes for an interesting, if not surprising, contrast. The B&I saw the workforce halved and wages cut by twenty per cent, and talk was of 'survival plans' in an atmosphere hostile to public enterprise and where the future of the national economy, never mind a shipping company, seemed at stake. The 1984 give-away of Sealink – described by the NUS as the 'Sale of the Century' – created all sorts of precedents and pressures. Privatisation brought crew reductions, worsened conditions and the continuous threat of cheaper, foreign crews. Irish seamen on the Irish sea were becoming an endangered species.

Not a Minister for Fish and Chips But a Minister for Shipping

Led by Barney Crossan, Terry Clare and Sean McCourt, the Irish Congress of Trade Unions adopted a raft of motions that outlined the crucial elements for an Irish maritime policy. Congress demanded the establishment of an Irish deep-sea and tanker fleet under an Irish flag. They want worker participation within any emerging company and improved worker representation on ferry safety committees. Flags of Convenience should be tightly controlled and a permit system to discriminate in favour of Irish and EU nationals in home waters introduced, together with the extension of the EU Directives on the Organisation of Working Time and Posting of Workers to seamen. The Irish maritime industry is in danger of total disappearance. What other domestic industry with such actual and employment potential would be disregarded in this manner?

Terry Clare offered derision to the politician who, when given a marine portfolio, said he was 'Minister for Fish & Chips'. 'We don't want a Minister for Fish & Chips,' said Clare, 'we want a Minister for Shipping.' Sean McCourt stated that marine transport 'accounts for

99 per cent of all Ireland's imports and exports' but with so few merchant ships 'it becomes abundantly clear that Ireland is largely reliant upon foreign flag vessels'. The current debate on Irish neutrality is incomplete without a proper discussion of such dependence. Commitments have been given about a minimum Irish merchant fleet but they have been ignored. Congress adopted all marine motions with acclaim but whether anyone has been listening is debatable.

The Coming of the ITF and a Warning to All Shipping

The increasing incidence of unpaid, Third World crews appearing on vessels of dubious seaworthiness in Irish ports is an obvious effect of Flags of Convenience and the virtual slave conditions of many East European, Asian and African seafarers. Support was always given by Irish trade unions but in a piecemeal and uncoordinated manner. In 2001 a meeting of all marine unions in SIPTU College led to the appointment of Tony Ayton as International Transport Workers' Federation Inspector for Ireland. It was reported recently that Ireland was second bottom of the European league table for inspections under the Port-State Control regulations, so the new ITF Office in Waterford is not short of work in trying to implement the 'Uniform TCC Collective Agreement for Crews on Flags of Convenience Ships'.

The underlying problem is the absence of an effective European Union maritime policy that will defend traditional European seafaring jobs at decent wages and conditions, respect our collective maritime cultures and recognise the significant contribution to the continent's trade and coastal environment that well-trained, highly motivated and properly rewarded crews could make. Michael Hayes of SIPTU is working closely with sister maritime unions to extend United Kingdom legislation concerning work permits for seafarers to Irish ports. This will give priority to EU nationals. SIPTU continues to campaign for the restoration of an Irish merchant fleet and is appalled by the lack of training and investment in what should be a dynamic industry. Everyone hails the Celtic Tiger but few recognise that it is a sea-borne phenomenon. John de Courcy Ireland asks, how much is being spent on foreign shipping and agents and can this cash not be directed to create and sustain a viable Irish merchant fleet?

So, Irish seafarers have a long history of organisation and struggle. They were central to the emergence of a 'New Unionism' with a socialist perspective. They were at the heart of the 1913 Lock Out, an episode that should be re-assessed for its maritime significance. The internationalism of seamen's trade unionism was seen in the heroic food ships and the fluttering emblem of the National Transport Workers' Federation on the steamship *Hare*. The defence of Irish shipping and cross-channel ferry routes – passenger and freight – have been at the centre of trade union demands that went beyond narrow concerns for wages and conditions to express concern for the nation's strategic interests in economic well-being, genuine neutrality and independence, and the safety, health and welfare of passengers and our coastal environment. Today, the seafarers' unions seek to defend all mariners through ITF agreements. It has been – and remains – a constant battle against a never slacking tide of public and political indifference.

In thinking again of faithful and courageous ordinary seamen like Benny Malone, stoker on Irish Shipping, is to consider thousands of similar tales of quiet dedication for little reward and less respect. Seamen's trade unions have never been numerically strong. They have been charged with corruption and internal mismanagement and they have been riven by dissent. But they have survived tremendous odds. Their opponents have been powerful, international shipping interests, national and European Governments. They have developed a unique solidarity nonetheless, served their members' interests well and presented to the broad labour movement and the political parties a maritime policy that requires action – and requires action now. A warning to all Irish shipping is that unless trade union policies are adopted, there will very shortly be no Irish shipping and no one will be better off for that eventuality.

13

Modern Commercial Antarctic Whaling

Rorke Bryan

An extract from Ordeal by Ice – Ships of the Antarctic by Rorke Bryan

M odern commercial whaling in Antarctica originated in the exploratory whaling voyages of the 1890s and the Nordenskjöld expedition on Antarctica. The moving spirit was the great Norwegian whaling skipper, C. A. Larsen. On his way back from the Antarctic expedition in 1904 Larsen convinced a business consortium in Buenos Aires to set up the Compañía Argentina de Pesca (PESCA) to establish a whaling station at Grytviken on South Georgia, with himself as resident manager. South Georgia lay within the Falkland Island Dependencies and the establishment of the whaling station generated considerable bureaucratic confusion and diplomatic angst.

The British government had claimed territorial rights over South Georgia since Captain Cook's voyage on *HMS Resolution* but had never exercised these actively. Matters came to a head in 1905 when the South Georgia Exploring Company, formed by British subjects in Punta Arenas, obtained a two-year lease from the Governor of the Falkland Islands to herd sheep on South Georgia. Arriving in Cumberland Bay on the schooner *Consort* with their livestock, they found

Larsen's whaling operation in full and, they claimed, illegal action. A flurry of diplomatic correspondence and a visit to Grytviken by the British warship *HMS Sappho* followed, its commander Captain Hodges allegedly giving Larsen fifteen minutes to haul down offending flags before opening fire. Ultimately, agreement was reached and a lease was signed between PESCA and the government of the Falkland Islands in March 1906. Amongst the terms of the lease was the establishment of a meteorological station at Grytviken. This became the responsibility of the Argentinian government in 1907 and was later used to support Argentinian territorial claims. In the next few years fourteen whaling leases were signed by British authorities for the waters around South Georgia, the South Orkneys, the South Shetlands, Heard Island and the Falklands.

The confrontation between Britain, Argentina and Norway forced British authorities to take its territorial claims seriously, leading several decades later to the voyages of the 'Discovery Investigations' to collect the data required for whale management. After issuing a lease to PESCA, in October 1906 the Falkland Islands government started to regulate whaling. Initially royalties were charged for each whale caught but, after complaints by whaling companies, these were replaced by set fees for the establishment of a land whaling station or floating factory ship. Later regulations limited wasteful use of whales (initially PESCA used less than 50 per cent of each whale) and imposed a closed season from late May to mid-September. In 1909 a resident magistrate was appointed to South Georgia to administer these regulations (and to act as shipping master, customs officer, postmaster, police commissioner and gaoler).

Larsen purchased most of the stores and equipment required from his home port of Sandefjord for the whaling operation at Grytviken. These included two prefabricated wooden buildings, one for cookers, blubber presses, boilers and a cooper's workshop, and the other as a residence. He also ordered a new whale catcher, the *Fortuna*, constructed for 95,000 Nkr (£5,400/$27,150) at Framnaes mek. Verk.

in Sandefjord. In 1904 steam whale catchers belonged to a relatively new class of ship; the first catcher built at Sandefjord by Framnaes mek. Verk. was *Ornen* in 1902 for Christen Christensen. The first true catcher, *Spes et Fides*, had been built in 1862 for Svend Foyn of Tønsberg who revolutionised whaling methods around Norway. Whaling had traditionally concentrated on relatively slow-moving species such as the sperm, right and humpback whales, which by the mid-nineteenth century were very scarce in northern waters. Fast, manoeuvrable, steam whale catchers made it possible to hunt the more abundant, faster-swimming rorquals, such as blue, fin and sei whales, which sink on death if not pumped with compressed air. Whale catcher design evolved quickly but the key features remained small size, speed, shallow draught and extreme manoeuvrability, together with sufficient power to tow five or six whales simultaneously.

To cope with the extreme conditions of the Southern Ocean, *Fortuna* was made significantly larger and stronger than *Ornen*: 164 grt (43 tons net), 30.34 m (99.5 feet) length, 6.10 m (20 feet) beam and 3.96 m (13 feet) draught. For her size, she had a powerful triple expansion steam engine of 280 ihp, which gave a maximum speed of 10 knots, and her greater size allowed a larger coal bunker capacity of 90 tons. Otherwise, she was typical of evolving catcher design, with a very fine hull cross-section, significant sheer (about 5.5 per cent), an elliptical counter stern and rounded bow like most trawlers, and a high bow where a harpoon gun was mounted. There was a crow's-nest on the mainmast and an open midships bridge with a small chart room over a galley and mess, while twelve crew were accommodated in the fo'c'sle and there was a small saloon aft. The waist was very low so, at speed in rough seas, the main deck was usually awash. Until after the Second World War, no whale catcher was fitted with a bilge keel and they rolled and pitched ferociously; Swinhoe (the leader of the South Georgia Exploring Company party) discovered these attributes during a short trip on *Fortuna* when her rapid, erratic

movements made him violently ill. Some catchers could turn 360°
in just over a minute, though this could be hazardous, particularly
if they were badly iced up or had partially full fuel tanks; and some,
like Salvesen's *Simbra* in 1947, capsized while turning.

Fortuna was launched in July 1904. Larsen also purchased two
ships to act as transports, the 371-ton (340 tons net), three-masted,
wooden barquentine *Rolf*, built by C. Sorensen at Arendal in 1885,
and the 1,065-ton (1,015 tons net), three-masted, wooden barque *Louise*, built as the Jennie S. Barker at Freeport, Maine, in 1869, but most
recently serving in the Baltic timber trade. *Louise* and *Fortuna* reached
Grytviken on 16 November followed by *Rolf* on 28 December. The
first whale was harpooned on 27 November but the processing plant
was not completed until just before Christmas. The weather was
very severe but abundant whales were found in the sheltered Cumberland Bay. In the first year 236 whales were caught, of which 80
per cent were humpbacks. The main product was oil, processed in
open cookers, then transferred to oak barrels for transport, but ba-
leen was also produced from humpback, right, blue and fin whales. A
first cargo of 165 tonnes (922 barrels) of oil together with whalebone
was transported by *Rolf* to Buenos Aires in February 1905. Net income for the complete first year of operation (15 December 1904 to 31
December 1905) was 83,256 pesos (£16,600/$83,000) with an average
price of £15.24 ($76.20) per ton for oil and £188 ($940) per tonne for
whalebone.

From *Ordeal by Ice – Ships of the Antarctic* by Rorke
Bryan, published by The Collins Press, www.col-
linspress.ie.

14

Queen Elizabeth Visits
the English Market

Pat O'Connell

Pat O'Connell, the legendary fishmonger from Cork's English Market, has been a regular guest on Seascapes down through the years. Below he describes the preparations for, and the historic visit of, Queen Elizabeth to the English Market.

In early 2011, Cork was awash with rumours that President Obama was likely to come to University College Cork during his trip to Ireland later that year. To put a plan in place for the expected visit, Cork City Council and UCC worked closely together. However, it soon became obvious that the President's visit to Ireland was going to be extremely brief and that fitting a Cork stopover into to such a tight schedule was totally out of the question.

One day, Paul Moynihan, a senior executive officer in corporate affairs with Cork City Council, had a light bulb moment and suggested to the Lord Mayor, Michael O'Connell, that since a lot of preparation had already been done in the hope that President Obama would visit Cork, Queen Elizabeth II should be invited to the city, especially as the queen had also planned a trip to Ireland during that year. The Lord Mayor sent out the invitation and got a reply within a week to say that the queen would be delighted to visit Cork during her state visit here. Her visit would be the first by a British monarch to the Republic of Ireland since the visit of King George V in 1911, when the whole island of Ireland was still under British rule.

Of course, the minute word of the visit got out, rumour and counter-rumour spread like wildfire. In all, about fifteen places were mentioned as possible locations for a royal visit, among them City Hall, UCC, Cobh and the English Market. Word had it that the queen had already received a present of *Serving a City*, the incredible story of the English Market, painstakingly put together by the O'Driscoll brothers, and that she was keen to visit the market. Naturally, taking into consideration our troubled past as neighbours, everyone began to wonder what kind of reception the queen would receive, or indeed if she would be welcome at all. In his day, my father would have been very much republican in his views. Mam may have looked at things differently, as most of her brothers had worked and lived in England for long spells. Personally, although I think that we are clearly very much shaped by our past, I don't believe for a minute that we should dwell on it. We are a young, educated country, a strong democracy with a young population and we are more than capable of holding our own with any nation. If what we do today makes a genuine difference and improves relations with our neighbours, then let's not be prisoners of our past. We must learn the lessons of our history, but we must make decisions based on our present and future.

One busy Friday afternoon, having just stepped outside our counter to speak to a customer who had recently been unwell, I suddenly found myself in the midst of a large group of very well-dressed people, about thirty in all, led by Paul Moynihan, who was an employee of Cork City Council. Paul introduced me to Edward Young, deputy private secretary to the queen. We all had a chat and a laugh before the group moved on. What had become a rumour now became very much a reality, and the first thought to enter my head at that moment was, what would Mam think if she knew that Queen Elizabeth II was now likely to visit her stall? At last, the English Market would have the chance to shine to a huge international audience and showcase Ireland's finest fish, meat, fruit, cheeses, vegetables and breads. Although as yet we had no idea what form the visit would take, I hoped that it could be carried off without changing the very character of the market.

After that Friday afternoon, the wheels began to quickly turn. Soon, we learned that the queen would touch down at Cork Airport and visit the English Market, along with the Tyndall National Institute at UCC, which is Ireland's leading microelectronics research centre. The timeframe for both the preparation for the visit and for the visit itself was tight.

Over the coming days and weeks, City Hall set up a series of meetings with traders, An Garda Síochána, Bord Bia, Bord Fáilte and public relations personnel. Paul Moynihan and his colleague Valerie O'Sullivan, a director of services in corporate and external affairs, took a hands-on approach to the planning and organisation of the Cork leg of the trip. The individual traders whose stalls the queen would visit learned of their selection only a few days before the visit. However, from the moment I heard of the visit, I worked on the basis that our stall would be one of those chosen. If it was, we would be prepared. If not, so be it.

For the next month, I prepared for the day of the royal visit. As I've said before, Castletownbere has been very good to our business down through the years. Truly, I believe their fish is among the best in the world. And if we were picked to showcase Irish fish to the world on the day of the visit, then O'Connell's would not be found wanting. For me, it was also important to show the character and tradition of the market, because for centuries, in this little space in the middle of Cork city, everything has changed and yet nothing has changed.

For years, I'd had a copy of a black and white photo taken in the market of Sheehan's fish stall sometime around 1910, showing the two Sheehan brothers who ran the stall, along with their wives and a young child, aged around ten, whom I assume was one of their sons. I got the photo enlarged to about seven feet in height and about fourteen feet in length. My thinking was that, in many ways, the photograph depicted a lot of what is and has been the ethos of the market down through the years – family-run businesses, superb product, hard work and lots of character.

With about two weeks to go to the visit, the market showed a noticeable increase in activity. Bord Bia, Bord Fáilte and An Garda Síochána were now very visible and constantly engaging with the traders and City Council. All of these worked closely with the traders' committee. Due to the short timespan allowed for the preparation, the committee, and its chairman Tom Durcan in particular, were on call around the clock. Peter Kelly – better known as Franc and famous for his wedding programme on RTÉ – was invited in to add a little colour and imagination to the duller areas of the market, though he was under strict instructions not to interfere with its very essence. His imagination, touch and subtlety worked a treat, from placing full grown trees in grey areas to decorating the fountain with a fabulous array of vegetables. Parts of the market that had been hidden away suddenly came to life.

On the Friday before the queen's visit, I got a phone call from Paul Moynihan saying that our stall had been selected as one of the stalls the queen would visit and asking me to attend a meeting on Monday morning in City Hall. My reaction, of course, was what would Kathleen O'Connell have thought had she received that phone call, the woman who had left South Presentation Convent at primary level, took a huge gamble on opening a small fish stall, and that very same stall was now going to receive a visit from Queen Elizabeth II? The other stalls chosen were Ashley O'Neill, butchers; The Farmer, fruit and vegetables; Isabelle Sheridan, cheese and delicatessen; Jerry Moynihan, poultry and eggs; Sheila Fitzpatrick, breads; and Toby Simmonds, olives. The excitement and apprehen-

Fishmonger Pat O'Connell in the English Market
(photo by Marcus Connaughton)

sion around the market was palpable. We were informed that only family and staff would be allowed in on the day and all these people had to fill in questionnaires, which would then be vetted by the relevant authorities.

For the previous five weeks, Paul and I had worked towards the expectation that our stall would probably be one of those the queen would visit. The fact that the expectation would now become a reality started to set off panic attacks. Would we have the fish we needed on the day? How would the visit be received in Cork? And, of course, what the hell do you chat about to the queen? Unfortunately, my knowledge of horses is zilch and I wasn't sure how much the queen knew about fish. Not a great starting point, really.

On Monday, the seven stall holders chosen to meet the queen arrived at City Hall as arranged. There, we met the lord mayor Michael O'Connell, Tim Lucey the city manager, an official from the British Embassy, Valerie O'Sullivan, Paul Moynihan and members of An Garda Síochána. We were told about the order of the queen's visit, the entrance through which she would arrive, areas where presentations would be made, lengths of the visit and the time she would spend at each stall. Also, we were informed of the protocol involved, part of which suggested that we would stand behind our counters while speaking to the queen. Sheila Fitzpatrick and I objected to this, as we felt that greeting the queen from behind the counter would create an immediate barrier. For my part, if I was showcasing Irish fish, I wanted to be able to pick up the different varieties of fish, not only to show them to the queen, but also to the worldwide audience looking on. We were told that it would be highly unlikely that we would be allowed to speak to the queen from outside the counter. But thirty minutes later, after a review of the situation, we were told that one trader at each of the selected stalls could stand outside the counter to greet the queen. Even then, I sensed that this was a hugely important decision.

Over the next few days, arrangements were put in place for bringing in stock before Friday, the day of the visit, as only people who had been vetted and had identity cards on the day would be allowed in. That week, security was tight and everyone was busy putting the final pieces in place. From a personal point of view, the pressure was intense. I suppose, compared to other products available in the market, ours is the most volatile supply-wise. We are weather dependent and also need a bit of luck with regards to the right catch on any given day. As it turned out, on that particular week, luck was on our side. On Thursday, the day before the visit, our fridge was heaving with the best fish this country has to offer, from stunning cod to perfect prawns.

At 5.30 p.m., members of An Garda Síochána carried out a security check on all the stalls, fridges and offices in the market. As our fridge was literally full to the brim, it meant that they had to empty the fridge first, check the boxes and then refill it. As Paul opened the fridge, he said to the three gardaí present, 'Ye really picked the short straw here lads.' I have to say, their professionalism was a credit to the force. But throughout the entire preparation, that was the case with everyone involved.

At 6.30 p.m., on the eve of the queen's visit, all the English Market traders closed their stalls and left the market as requested. I went home, looking forward to a good night's rest. But it wasn't to be, as I never slept a wink.

The night before the visit had turned out to be frustrating. All night long, I twisted and turned. My mind refused to relax. Deep down, what was really bothering me of course was the fact that there would be no re-takes, no second chances. In the English Market, the traders are well used to being in front of cameras. But the big difference this time was that there would be only one opportunity to get it right. I would have only three or four minutes with the queen. The world would be watching and watching closely. If anything went wrong, there would be no chance to say, 'We'll re-do that last piece.'

During the previous week, I'd obviously considered the possibilities of how my conversation with the queen might go. The trouble was that I had no idea what the queen was like. If I'm honest, she always struck me as being somewhat dour, with no sense of humour. In hindsight, that's what was niggling me most, because to try to create the right atmosphere and ambience of the market, I needed someone with a sense of humour.

At 7.00 a.m. next morning, as I drove to the English Market, all of this was going through my mind. The only gate open at the market was the one at Oliver Plunkett Street. Security was intense. First, I was given a printed badge, showing my name and the name of our stall. Then I had to enter through a scanner, like the one used at airports. I was searched and whatever I was carrying was checked. Again, though, the whole process was professional, efficient and courteous.

Soon, Paul arrived, followed by Liz, Denis, Emma, Seán and Kris. Normally on Fridays, we start somewhere between 6.30 and 7.00 a.m., bringing in fish, loading the counters, filleting and preparing orders. However, this particular Friday had a strange, surreal feeling about it. The fish had been brought in the previous evening, with the exception of some wild salmon which to my delight had arrived that very morning. We had no orders and no filleting, and we didn't want to fill the counters up until 11.00 a.m. to make sure that every fish looked in pristine condition. Paul, Liz, Denis, Kris and I wore our normal, cotton chefs' jackets, blue aprons, white hats and wellingtons. For Emma and Seán, we had something a little different. On the day before, we had hung the giant mural of the Sheehan family in the 1900s over our freezers at the end of the stall. To match the clothes worn by those in the photo, Emma wore a long, black dress and a white, cotton bib, while Seán dressed in a tweed cap, a waistcoat with a black back and tweed front, a collarless, striped shirt and tweed pants. To further mirror the picture, we filled old-style lobster pots with masses of seaweed and topped them off with Castletownbere's finest prawns. Also, we matched the display of white fish in the picture and decided that Emma and Seán should stand in front of the photo, with the matching display of fish before them. Everything changes and yet nothing changes.

About 11.00 a.m., we packed the main counters with ice and began to put our display together. This was very much Paul's responsibility as he has a wonderful eye for arranging fish and colour, which is probably why he is such a great photographer. My job had been to source the fish. Paul's job was to display it. Over the next few hours, under the watchful eye of Paul, everyone worked together to create a really stunning array of local, fresh fish, mostly from Castletownbere, all fit for a queen and displayed in a fashion to make the rest of the world envious of the bounty we have surrounding this island of ours – huge prawns, beautiful turbot, hake, lemon sole, plaice, mackerel, oysters, live crab and lobster, haddock, gurnard, monkfish and whiting. We topped it all off with lovely wild salmon from the River Lee and organic salmon from Bantry.

At this stage, the market was buzzing, with the stall holders fussing and double checking to make sure everything was shipshape. Bord Bia were giving advice to stall holders on final tweaks to the displays. Everywhere, cameras were flashing. The sense of anticipation was palpable. RTÉ were busy getting cameras into position, with the lighting having been put in the previous week. Security personnel were hovering around in large numbers, scrutinising every single detail.

About 1.00 p.m., RTÉ did a practice walk through the route the queen would take, to make sure that their camera angles and lighting were correct. They had to get it right as they were the feed for the other television stations showing the event and their coverage was going out worldwide. For the trial run, one of their producers, Marie Toft, picked the short straw to play the part of the queen. Accompanied by the lord mayor and several others, she followed the official route the queen would take in less than an hour. The group stopped at each of the stalls the queen would visit and tried to imitate the walk-through as best they could. Marie played the part of the queen to perfection, or at least it matched my perception of what the queen would be like – very formal, very straitlaced, aloof, without any sense of humour. If the real queen was indeed like this, my Cork wit and irreverence would go down like a lead balloon. Later, I tried to speak to one of the producers, to spell out my concerns, but it was impossible to get near any of the crew at this stage, as they were run off their feet. So, what should I do – go frightfully formal or Cork cheeky?

Paul turned on the computer. By now, the queen was being driven through the South Mall, just around the corner from the Grand Parade entrance through which she would enter the market, and the streets were thronged with people. Behind our counter, we were joined by Claire O'Sullivan of the *Irish Examiner*, P.J. Coogan from the local radio station 96FM, two photographers from England, including the royal photographer, Arthur Edwards (some of his amazing photographs are in this book), and an RTÉ camera man.

Within minutes, Queen Elizabeth II was approaching our stall, having stopped and chatted at the stall of Ashley O'Neill, the first of the seven traders selected to meet her. 'Your Majesty, *céad míle fáilte* to Cork's English Market,' says I, knowing that the queen's Irish was very good, having heard her televised speech at Dublin Castle on the previous night. Strangely enough, now I wasn't the slightest bit nervous – guess it was going to be Cork cheeky.

First, I introduced the queen to Emma and Seán and told her a little about the picture behind them. Again, I was trying to emphasise the fact that, in a place like the English Market where traditional influences are so strong, everything changes, yet nothing really changes. Then, I began to show her the huge variety of fish on display, as the two of us walked slowly down the fish aisle with the Lord Mayor and Lady Mayoress, followed by Prince Philip, Simon

The Queen showing she has a sense of humour

Coveney, Kathleen Lynch, Tim Lucey, a large entourage from City Council and an English delegation.

One of the first fish to catch the queen's eye was a large monkfish and the queen was quick to ask what it was. Now, in Cork we sometimes call this the mother-in-law fish, but this was about a week after the royal wedding of William and Kate. So, because of the person I was speaking to and because the world was looking on, and because I was in some ways representing the English Market, the city and the fish industry, I had to be diplomatic, didn't I? You must be joking, boy!

'That, Your Majesty, is what we in Cork call a mother-in-law fish.' As I said earlier, my perception of the queen was that she didn't have a great sense of humour. Boy, did I get that one wrong. She thought it was hilarious. Now Cork cheekiness was on a roll.

Next to the monkfish, Paul had arranged a gorgeous turbot. Apparently, the queen had turbot for lunch the day before in Dublin and, when I mentioned this to her, she must have wondered how I knew, but living in a small country like Ireland, word tends to travel fast. Beside the turbot lay the crème de la crème, wild salmon from our own River Lee. I took great pride in explaining to the queen that the salmon had been caught that very morning in the Lee by Simon Quilligan, a local fisherman. The salmon was in prime condition, glistening under the lights as only wild salmon can, with crimson red gills. I suppose this to me was exactly what sets the market apart as, not only could I tell the queen about the type of fish on display, but I could also say where, when and how it was caught. So there was no need to describe it as a produce of Ireland, or produced in Ireland. No, boy. This was pure Cork. The queen listened intently and seemed hugely impressed that a river running through a city the size of Cork could be clean enough to maintain such fabulous fish. Cork City Council take a bow.

While we chatted about the wild salmon, I also showed the queen organic salmon from Bantry Bay, superb in quality and appreciated all over the world. But there are big differences between wild and organic salmon, especially in relation to texture and quality.

At this stage, we were moving on to a big mound of Dublin Bay prawns, which were select prawns from one of the Castletownbere trawlers. They were absolutely massive. As I picked up several of these to show to the queen, I had a bit of a lightbulb moment myself and said, 'Your Majesty, I'll let you in on a little secret. This week, it's my thirtieth wedding anniversary and the last time I was this nervous was thirty years ago.'

'But you are all right now,' she answered, before throwing her head back in a fit of laughter. That moment was captured on camera by the photographer Valerie O'Sullivan and became one of the most iconic images of the queen's visit to Ireland – and of course ideal for the cover of this memoir!

Behind the prawns, Paul had laid some large Red Gurnard, which because of their fierce-looking head and orangey-red colour are really striking. They impressed the queen so much that she called Prince Philip closer to show them to him. We chatted for a few minutes about the gurnard before finally moving on to our own smoked salmon. Obviously, I got huge pleasure and satisfaction in telling Queen Elizabeth about our smoke-house in Bandon and it was a lovely way to end the queen's visit to our stall.

I held out my hand, we shook hands and I wished her well. Then, I sighed the biggest sigh of relief in my entire life and thought, Kathleen, we did well.

From *The Fishmonger*, by Pat O'Connell, published by The Liffey Press, www.theliffeypress.com

L.E. Samuel Beckett (courtesy of Irish Defence Forces)

15

The Irish Naval Service

John Kavanagh

Commodore John Kavanagh is the Former Flag Officer Commanding the Irish Naval Service. The essay below is from one of the six Thomas Davis Lectures that aired on Seascapes on RTÉ Radio 1.

U p to the time of Ireland achieving its independence from Great Britain, the only Navy which frequented the waters around our coast and our ports was the British or Royal Navy. Even after receiving our independence, under the terms of the 1921 Treaty, the new Free State could not raise its own Naval Force. Britain was still to remain entirely responsible for the naval defence of our shores. It also retained the right to continued use of the key ports at Berehaven, Cork Harbour and Lough Swilly. While the formation of a Navy was not permitted under the Treaty, a fledgling Fishery Protection Service was established in 1922 which consisted of a hotch-potch collection of armed trawlers and an ex-Royal Navy tug. That this embryonic Service was allowed to disband only ten months after its creation speaks volumes about the attitude of the new Irish State to its maritime circumstances.

During the inter-war period, the Irish Free State took little interest in the country's maritime affairs. Our harbours and ports were allowed to deteriorate and the former coastguard stations were sold off or left derelict.

The lighthouse and buoyance system around the Irish coast which had been established under British rule continued to be maintained. While a Marine Rescue Coordination Organisation was established to oversee Search and Rescue, a coastguard was not formed until the early 1990s!

While other small maritime countries were building up and protecting coastal and deep-sea fishing industries, Ireland was left with only one antiquated patrol boat called the *Murchú* which was totally inadequate for the job of fishery protection. Prior to World War II the *Murchú* operated with the Department of Agriculture and was taken over by the Marine and Coast watching Service for wartime patrols. So in 1938 when the British Army and Royal Navy evacuated the ports and seas around Ireland, the country was left totally unprepared to defend its neutrality status which had been declared at the outbreak of World War II. The implications for Ireland were serious. Lying to the West of Britain and straddling that country's main supply lines Ireland was vulnerable to attack from either side if possession of Irish ports was deemed to be necessary for the control of the Western approaches. Without a Navy the country was not in a position to fulfil the minimum requirements of a neutral state under the terms of the Hague Convention. This deficiency was very quickly identified by the Intelligence Section in Defence Force headquarters which advised the government that to protect our seaborne trade and control our territorial seas the State would require a fleet consisting of a light cruiser, five destroyers, a sloop, ten anti-submarine craft, two fleet tankers, backed up by coastal patrol boats, mine layers and mine sweepers, not to mention two shore bases at Haulbowline and Dun Laoghaire. Submarines were subsequently added to this list escalating the costs still further. The cost of such a fleet would have been enormous, so the government wanted what was known as 'a more realistic approach' to be taken. After much toing and froing with regard to choice of vessels, six motor torpedo boats were acquired from the Royal Navy between 1940 and 1942. These craft coupled with the antiquated *Murchú* and the *Fort Rannoch* made up the sea going elements of the Marine and Coast Watching Service for the duration of the war. The motor torpedo boats, while having a high speed at 35 knots, were only 72 feet in length and were quite unsuited for sea conditions around the Irish coast, and in particular off the southwest and west coasts. The crisis at the outbreak of World War II had found this country almost defenceless. The Defence Forces when mobilised were inadequate in size and were poorly trained and equipped. There was very little public perception of the problems and responsibilities arising from the adoption of neutrality, nor indeed was there any great realisation of a possibility of a threat of invasion. At the end of the war it was obvious that the lack of even a nucleus of a naval force was an omission that should never again be permitted.

On 15 March 1946 the Government decided that the Wartime Marine Service should become a permanent component of the Defence Forces and that the maritime inscription should become the naval reserve, or the Slua Muiri as it was to be called. The title naval service was formally adopted in November 1946 – this date can be taken as the birth of the new Irish Navy or of the current Navy. It was decided to purchase six flower class corvettes from the Royal Navy but this was later reduced to three, principally due to a shortage of man power. The intention was to take delivery of a further three vessels two years later. This idea was scrapped, again because of the continuing shortage of trained man power. These 1,000-ton vessels were built at the beginning of the war for convoy escort duties. The three vessels acquired by the new naval service were built in 1942 and were renamed the *Macha*, *Maev* and *Cliona*. Powered by triple expansion, steam reciprocating engines, they could manage a speed of 16 knots. They had open bridges – in other words, you didn't have a roof over your head while on watch. This meant that during your four hours on the bridge you were exposed to the elements as well as the occasional dollop of sea water with very little shelter. For protection, one was issued with tarry oil skins, southwesters, sea-boots and duffle coats. The corvettes also had a tendency to move about a lot (and I mean a lot). Even a moderate swell on the west coast could induce 30 to 40 degree rolls. Someone once stated that corvettes would roll in a 'wet field'. Life onboard these ships was accurately depicted in Nicholas Monsarrat's book *The Cruel Sea*, which was made into a highly successful movie. Having joined the Navy in early 1959, I experienced life on all three corvettes during the remaining 10 years of their service.

My first experience of an overseas trip was in 1960, when *L.E. Cliona* was directed to proceed to Antwerp. The purpose of the trip was to collect the first consignment of FN rifles for use by the Army about to proceed on United Nations duty in the Congo. The *Cliona*, with its cargo of rifles and ammunition, berthed at the North Wall in Dublin. The weapons were transported directly to Dublin Airport and, shortly afterwards, a US Globemaster flew overhead bearing the first troops armed with FN rifles to the Congo.

The Navy thus for the first time provided the vital re-supply service to our early UN missions overseas. Living ashore it is hard to realise what naval personnel could experience in bad weather. When a hurricane hit Ireland in September of 1961, the corvette *L.E. Cliona* was anchored in Killybegs Harbour. A forecast came through of a very severe storm approaching the west coast of Ireland. (The vessel was under the command of Lt Commander Liam Moloney, later to become Flag Officer Commanding Naval Service and later still Assistant Chief of Staff.)

This soon was upgraded to hurricane force as Hurricane Debbie, which had originated in the Caribbean, was fast approaching the coast. Being at anchor in Killybegs, which is a fairly enclosed harbour, it was decided to weigh anchor, proceed to sea and ride out the storm in Donegal Bay. Indeed, it was a full-blown hurricane which caused much structural damage to buildings, trees, etc., ashore. Onboard *L.E. Cliona*, every canvas cover was either blown away or shredded, but otherwise the ship emerged unscathed. I do recall that it was virtually impossible to hear on the bridge given the shriek of the wind and the continuous wall of spray being driven along the surface and over the ship. On re-entering Killybegs, when the wind had abated, there was hardly an intact roof left in the town. As the sixties wore on the corvettes gradually wore out and were all decommissioned by 1970. During this period, they were used primarily for fishery protection. Back then, the country was still outside the EU, or the European Economic Community as it was then called, and we had jurisdiction only over a three-mile limit.

I can recall one case of a French lobster man arrested outside the Blasket Islands and a court case taking place that evening in Tralee. The District Justice found the skipper guilty and charged and fined him the princely sum of £20. Immediately, the skipper whipped off his cap and he and the rest of the crew put what money they had into the cap which was then solemnly handed to the court clerk. The clerk counted the money, all in French Francs, borrowed the Justice's *Irish Times* to check the rate of exchange, and then slipped a note to the bench. The District Justice proceeded to reduce the fine to £17-7-6.

On a sad note, two of the corvettes, *Macha* and *Cliona*, were involved in the search for the Aer Lingus Viscount which disappeared in the vicinity of the Tuskar Rock shortly after crossing the Irish coast in March 1967. A combined search by the Naval Service and Royal Navy recovered only a small percentage of the bodies and it took over a further two months before the main body of the wreckage was located. And so we had reached the end of the corvette era and replacement vessels had to be acquired in a hurry.

This was a particularly bleak period for the Navy with morale at a low ebb. There was a poor perception of the Navy among the public at large and a song at the time about the three corvettes which referred to the crews going home for their tea did not help matters.

For a brief period the fishery research vessel the *Cú Feasa* with an armed naval officer embarked was assigned to fishery protection duties when the service was left without ships. Various ship designs were inspected and, in 1971, the first contract for an offshore patrol vessel was signed with Verolme Cork Dockyard. The first of this class, *L.E. Deirdre*, was launched in January 1972 and commissioned in June of the same year, under the command of Lt Cdr Liam Brett (later to become Flag Officer Commanding Naval Service). However, between the decommissioning of the corvettes in 1969/1970 and the commissioning of *L.E. Deirdre* in June 1972, we had to fill this gap with some Naval vessels. Fortunately, at this time, the Royal Navy were disposing of a number of ton class coastal minesweepers.

I was part of the ships company which went to Portsmouth in early January 1971 where we set to work in de-preserving and storing the first of these vessels. By the end of January 1971, the ship was commissioned and named *L.E. Grainne*. Shortly thereafter, under the command of Lt Cdr Joe Deasy, later to become Commodore and Flag Officer, we sailed for Cork Harbour. I then joined up with the two ships companies assigned to the remaining two minesweepers which lay in Gibraltar. An Aer Lingus Viscount was chartered for the flight which did not go entirely to plan. At this time, the border crossing from Gibraltar to mainland Spain was closed over the ongoing dispute involving Spain's claim over the Rock. As Ireland, in purchasing two warships from the British in Gibraltar, was deemed to be fraternising with the opposition, the Aer Lingus flight was refused permission to fly through Spanish air space en route to Gibraltar. We had to be routed down over Portugal and approach the Rock from over Morocco, which made landing at Gibraltar airport even more precarious than usual. We spent about six weeks on the Rock de preserving and storing the two ships before they were commissioned and named *L.E. Banba* and *L.E. Fola*.

These two ships had originally served on the Royal Navy station in Hong Kong, and while they had been built in the 1950s had been laid up or mothballed for many years. When we first boarded them, they were a sorry sight on the outside as the local seagull population must have been particularly attracted to them. However, internally they were in excellent condition and we soon had them shipshape and ready to steam back to Ireland. While the accommodation on board was rather cramped compared to the later custom-built vessels, there was a very good *esprit de corps* among their crews and many servicemen of all ranks have fond memories of their service on board these ships.

Deirdre, the first vessel designed and built for the Navy, became operational in mid-1972, and I had the pleasure of serving as Executive Officer with the first crew. The commissioning of the first new vessel to be specifically designed and built for the Navy provided a much needed boost for the service with a consequential improvement in morale. The standard of training and service conditions for personnel also improved. During the 1970s a number of developments took place which had a major impact on the Navy. In January 1973, Ireland joined the European Economic Community as it was then called. The resultant Community Common Fisheries Policy followed the decision to introduce a community wide 200 mile exclusive economic zone which totally transformed and expanded the task of the Naval Service. We had moved from patrolling a three to twelve mile territorial sea to a 200 mile limit, an area equivalent to five times the land mass of Ireland. In order to cope with patrolling this vast area, orders soon followed for three more vessels of the *Deirdre* class which were somewhat modified from the original design. While in command of *L.E. Deirdre* in August 1979, I was on patrol west of Fastnet when a storm unexpectedly hit the Irish coast. This coincided with the Fastnet Race with a fleet of yachts stretching from Cowes to Fastnet Rock being caught out in a storm. By the time the wind abated, 23 yachts had been abandoned, 15 lives were lost and 139 sailors rescued. *L.E. Deirdre* spent five days searching the area between Fastnet and the Scilly Isles rendering assistance to a large number of yachts in distress. The Naval Service was to participate in many search and rescue incidents in the years to follow.

By 1980 the Naval Service had four of the *Deirdre* class in commission, *Emer*, *Aoife* and *Aisling* being added to the fleet after construction in Verolme Cork Dockyard. We still had the three minesweepers in commission so the Service was in a strong position of growth. In 1979, one of these vessels, *L.E. Emer* was dispatched to the Lebanon on a re-supply mission for the Irish UNIFIL Battalion and this was the first such mission which was repeated either once or twice annually up to the final Irish UNIFIL Battalion in the year 2001.

The end of 1984 was a black period in Irish maritime history. In November, Irish Shipping Ltd, the National Merchant Shipping Line, went into liquidation. The following month, in December, the only large shipbuilding facility in the country, Verolme Cork Dockyard, closed down. Though unconnected these two events had a significant negative impact on Ireland's status as a maritime state. The country's national shipping line was no more, nor was the shipyard that had built many of its largest ships, which indeed was a very sad state of affairs for a small island state. On a brighter note, in December 1984, the Naval Service took delivery of the helicopter patrol vessel, *L.E. Eithne*, the last ship to be built in Verolme Cork Dockyard, and this added a whole new dimension to the Service's capabilities. With an Aer Corps-manned Dauphin helicopter embarked, this vessel had the capacity to reach out to a large sea area in its fishery protection or search and rescue role. When in command of *Eithne* in 1989/90, I can recall one episode which clearly showed the value of having a helicopter embarked in the fishery protection role. While patrolling southwest of the Fastnet, the helicopter was directed to carry out a sweep to the south of the ship. Within minutes, the chopper had identified two fishing vessels fishing illegally below the horizon about 25 miles from *Eithne*. They were both quickly arrested and escorted to Castletownberehaven, appeared before a Justice, and fined a total of £60,000.

Other ship acquisitions in the 1980s included the two Peacock class fast-patrol boats purchased from the Royal Navy. These vessels, which had been based in Hong Kong, provided the Navy for the first time with fast ships capable of doing 26 knots. Having this speed capability made these vessels ideal for responding quickly to situations such as attempts to import arms or drugs. Indeed, in 1994, the first major drug seizure by the Naval Service involved one of these vessels, the *L.E. Orla*, seizing the yacht *Brime* off the west coast after a prolonged surveillance operation. Since then, a number of other such operations have been successfully carried out by the *Orla* and her sister ship *L.E. Ciara*.

The 1990s have brought many substantial changes to the Naval Service. A series of consecutive reviews into the organisation and roles of the Navy were finally concluded at the end of the decade. On completion of the investigation into the Defence Forces a White Paper was published in February 2000. As a consequence of these developments, Naval Headquarters was relocated to the Naval Base at Haulbowline, and a totally new organisation was introduced in 2000. The various reviews and the White Paper on Defence were by and large positive towards the Naval Service, and provided a focussed blueprint for future developments. The other major development was the construction of two state of the art large patrol vessels, *L.E. Roisín* and *L.E. Niamh*. These ships, built in Appledore Shipyard in North Devon, are almost as big as *L.E. Eithne* and have a speed of 23 knots.

The White Paper on Defence, among its many recommendations, identified the Naval Service as the single seagoing agency of the State which should be capable of responding to any emergency or policing tasks arising in the country's maritime zone. This zone, as well as encompassing our 12 mile territorial sea, the 200 mile exclusive fishing limit, also has jurisdiction over a designated portion of the Continental Shelf which is more than double that of the 200 mile zone.

The White Paper also acknowledges and includes a replacement programme for each of the existing fleet of older vessels as they complete their notional lifespan of 30 years' service. The first commitment to this programme was the replacement of *L.E. Deirdre* with *L.E. Niamh* when *Deirdre* was decommissioned and sold after 30 years' service. While fishery protection continues to be our main day to day task, our ships while on patrol may also be called upon to respond to any emergencies which may arise as well as taking action against illegal drug or arms importations. As a result, the Naval Service has geared itself up through training and the acquisition of specialised equipment to attempting to control the attempted importation of illicit drugs. In 1995 another major development took place in the Navy with the enlistment for the first time of female cadets into the Service; the first female recruits soon followed. There are now a number of fully qualified female watchkeeping officers serving aboard Naval Service ships. All ship and shore departments now have women working alongside their male colleagues, and their introduction and integration into the service has been an outstanding success. Because of the nature of life in the Naval Service there has always been a higher turnover of personnel than that of our sister services. Because of the technical qualifications attained by men and women in the service they are actively sought after by many of the companies operating in the Cork Harbour area. This results in a requirement for ongoing recruitment of recruits, cadets, direct entry officers and technicians.

However, the recent major recruitment campaign for the Defence Forces, coupled with the positive publicity from missions such as the *L.E. Niamh* Asian deployment, has seen a significant upswing in recruitment in all categories. Another current development for the Naval Service and for maritime education in Ireland is the confirmation and construction of a National Maritime College near the Naval

Base in Ringaskiddy. This institution will be managed in partnership between the Department of Nautical Studies in the Cork Institute of Technology and the Naval Service, and should give a significant boost to providing qualified personnel for the maritime sector in Ireland, both Naval and mercantile.

I believe that developments over the past few years have made the Naval Service a very capable and progressive service. Voyages to Canada, the USA and in particular the recent Asian deployment display that we have 'a very long reach' capacity both in ships and the personnel who man them. It means that the Government of the day has at its disposal a capability to project what is technically a piece of national territory anywhere in the world in furtherance of national policies. This could be in facilitating the expansion of our trade relations with other countries, as in the case of the recent Asian deployment. Providing Naval support in disaster relief or humanitarian missions are other possible future roles for the service. It is also conceivable that a role may be found for the Navy in future United Nations-mandated missions. The Naval Service has come a long way since the end of the 1960s when, for a brief period, the Navy had no ships. The development of the multi-role nature of the Naval Service, now copperfastened by the White Paper on Defence, has more than justified the existence of a Navy for this small maritime island state. I believe its future is secure providing a challenging career for young men and women interested in a life at sea.

The man from Annascaul – Tom Crean and his puppies
(photo by Frank Hurley, by kind permission of The Collins Press)

16

Cast Adrift

Michael Smith

An extract from An Unsung Hero: Tom Crean – Antarctic Survivor by Michael Smith

On the ice the men could hear the dying agonies of *Endurance* as the ship groaned and creaked under the weight of the immense pressure which slowly strangled the vessel in its vice-like hold. If the ship had been a living thing, someone would have ended her misery. Few managed a good night's sleep, partly because the ice floe beneath was constantly cracking and on three occasions they were forced to move the tents to a more secure-looking spot. Alongside the men were the three little boats which were lifted off the dying ship. They alone seemed to offer a tenuous chance of survival – if they could escape the ice and reach the open sea.

There were only five tents to accommodate the 28 men gathered together on the drifting ice floe as they sought shelter and comfort only 200 yards (182 m) from the doomed *Endurance*. Also there were only eighteen reindeer-fur sleeping bags and the unlucky ones had to sleep in woollen bags, which held the damp and offered less protection against the freezing temperatures. The unfortunate ten were wisely chosen by lot to avoid any unnecessary friction or claims of favouritism.

But Shackleton ensured that each tent had its own natural leader, aware that maintaining discipline and morale would be essential in the struggle ahead. A decline in morale could spread like wildfire and lead to anarchy. He chose leaders carefully and placed Crean in charge of Number Four, a small hoop tent which also contained two polar veterans, Marston and Cheetham, and the cheerful, banjo-playing meteorologist, Hussey.

Over the next few days, the men made repeated trips to rescue precious supplies and equipment from *Endurance* before she met her inevitable end. These were melancholic little excursions for the men who understandably saw the ship as their last link with civilisation. Psychologically the loss of the ship meant severing the umbilical cord and on one trek a party of men respectfully hoisted the Union Jack. At least the ship would go down with colours flying.

The men were ordered to prepare themselves for the coming journey across the ice and hopefully to the edge of the open sea, where they would launch the little boats. Crean had already arranged the packing of the sledges with as many rations as he could reasonably stow and along with others, he was also deployed on frequent trips to hunt for seals.

With a tough journey ahead, the men were issued with a completely new set of underwear, socks and Burberrys and asked to limit their personal possessions to a modest 2 lb (0.9 kg) in weight. It meant many heartbreaking choices as the men considered what to keep and what to throw away in the snow.

Shackleton emphasised that nothing was of value if it worked against their survival. As he spoke, he took out his own gold watch, gold cigarette case and a few gold sovereigns and theatrically tossed them into the snow. He then opened the Bible which Queen Alexandra had given the ship a little over a year earlier and tore out the flyleaf containing her personal message. He also ripped out a single page containing verse a from the Book of Job, which reads:

Out of whose womb came the ice?
And the hoary frost of Heaven, who hath gendered it?
The waters are hid as with a stone.
And the face of the deep is frozen.

There were exceptions. Hussey, for example, was ordered to keep his banjo even though it weighed about 12 lb (5.4 kg) because, as Shackleton explained, it was 'vital mental medicine'. The surgeons' medical instruments were kept for obvious reasons and those who kept diaries were allowed to hang onto them.

But all around them on the ice were scattered forlorn reminders of home and the ordinary trappings of a normal life – personal keep-sakes, books, clothes, plus more practical reminders of their original purpose, like scientific instruments, telescopes and carpenter's tools. Tom Crean kept the scapular around his neck.

Before they prepared to leave, Crean was called upon to administer a particularly grim chore. There was no room on the trek for those who could not pull their weight so three of Crean's carefully nurtured pups and Chips McNeish's popular cat, Mrs Chippy, were shot. It was Crean, who was so fond of animals, who executed the animals. Even a tough polar hand like Crean was affected by the unhappy, but necessary task and Worsley recalled:

'Macklin, Crean and Chips seem to feel the loss of their friends rather badly.'

It was decided to take only two of the three boats and the bulk of the gear was carefully loaded. Each boat, loaded with the vital food and supplies, was placed on specially prepared sledges and weighed nearly one ton (over 1,000 kg). With some trepidation, the party set out on Saturday 30 October.

It was obvious from the start that it would require prodigious effort to haul the boats across the tortured, broken landscape of ice hummocks which surrounded them on the drifting ice floe. A team of four man-haulers went ahead with picks and shovels, trying to smooth out the undulating surface and ease the path of the boat-pullers. There followed the dog teams pulling seven sledges, who went back and forth in a monotonous routine of relaying their dreadfully heavy loads. Behind them came fifteen men, yoked to the largest boat in a long sledging harness. After moving on a short distance, they regrouped and began the same process of hauling the smaller boat, which offered the prospect of only slightly lighter pulling.

The long procession of men, dogs, sledges and boats stretched for half a mile across the disturbed commotion of ice. They calculated that, at best, the most distance they could manage would be 5 miles (8 km) a day, which implied many weeks and possibly months of strenuous exertion to reach the safety of land or open seas. The cost in human effort would be enormous and another very real fear was that at any moment, the ice could open up and swallow them or separate them from the relative safety of their camp. Any realists in the party must have doubted their chances of survival.

The men received a painful reminder of their slim chances after the first back-breaking day in the wet, soft snow which made the going appalling. Occasionally the men sank to their waists in the soggy, slushy conditions. Each step was terribly heavy labour and after the most colossal effort, they were near to exhaustion when they stopped for the day.

To their utter dismay they discovered that they had covered barely one mile. They made the same distance on 31 October, arriving physically worn out after a day when they flogged themselves to the point of collapse. The next morning, the march was abandoned.

The 28 men were now camped on a sizeable, solid-looking floe about one mile across which offered some degree of stability in comparison with their ordeal during the slow death of Endurance. But they were still inside the Antarctic Circle, drifting slowly northwards on a chunk of ice which at any time might split apart. Shackleton appropriately named it 'Ocean Camp'.

The aim was to remain as comfortable as possible at Ocean Camp and let the floe travel gently northwards towards open seas before setting out in the boats to row for the safety of Paulet or Snow Hill Island off to the west. Since they had abandoned the march only 2 miles away from the broken hulk of Endurance, the men made repeated journeys back to retrieve supplies and equipment which might help sustain them through the coming months.

Two important decisions were taken at this time. First it was decided to return to the vicinity of the ship and recover the third small boat. Second, to bring back more lengths of timber and nails from the mother ship which would be used to build up the sides of the three small boats for the proposed journey across the ocean to dry land.

Wild also managed to bring back Endurance's wheelhouse which was modified to make a useful galley and storehouse on the ice. From the patchwork roof they defiantly flew the Union Jack which King George had given to Shackleton on the eve of departure from London.

It was also decided to rescue some of Hurley's precious and memorable photographs, mostly glass plates which had been stored in metal cases on Endurance, now over 3 ft (1 m) under the mushy ice. It was not possible to keep all 600 plates and camera equipment so Hurley sat on the ice and calmly assessed the merit of each picture. As a negative was rejected, he summarily smashed the plate, thus ensuring that there would be no second thoughts. However, he retained one small pocket camera and about 120 plates which contain some of the most outstanding Polar pictures ever taken and are a fine memorial to a truly great photographer.

Crean, meanwhile, ensured that the sledges were kept loaded and ready for instant departure in case of any break in the ice and others were sent on a daily search for penguins, seals or anything else that might be eaten. Fortunately, there were sufficient supplies in the vicinity, although Shackleton was anxious not to stockpile too much food. He reckoned that storing large supplies of seal and penguin meat would send out the wrong signals to the men, suggesting that they were prepar-ing to endure the unthinkable – another winter on the ice.

Above all, he wanted to keep up morale and hope. To counter any developing fears or loss of heart, Shackleton talked frequently about going home and the future expeditions on which they would all sail. He also moved Ocean Camp a little way onto firmer, more comfortable snow, which also helped make life a little more bearable.

The men filled their time with a mixture of duties like searching for food and maintaining the equipment, or alternatively with games of cards or a browse through the handful of books – like Encyclopaedia Britannica – which had been salvaged from Endurance. At night the twang of Hussey's banjo – the 'mental medicine' – could be heard drifting across the eerie landscape.

In early November, temperatures began to revive which was a mixed blessing. It was warmer but it also meant that the area around Ocean Camp became a slushy, waterlogged mess, with men's feet frequently sinking deep into the morass. Everything was wet through.

There was almost a sense of relief when, on 21 November, Endurance finally succumbed to the Antarctic. At around 5 p.m., Shackleton suddenly called out, 'She's going, boys' and everyone scrambled to snatch a final farewell to their ship. She went down, bows first, her stern raised in the air before the ice swallowed the broken vessel.

From *An Unsung Hero: Tom Crean – Antarctic Survivor* by Michael Smith, published by The Collins Press, www.collinspress.ie

17

Ireland's Maritime Heroes

Marcus Connaughton

Marcus Connaughton is the Producer/Presenter of Seascapes on RTÉ Radio 1. The article below is from a speech he gave at the Burren Law School in Ballyvaughn, County Clare in 2013, and again later that year in the boardroom of The Port of Cork for Heritage Week.

From a maritime perspective this country's place among the nations of the world is a formidable one for a small island nation on the periphery of Western Europe. My first memory of being conscious of the sea and far-flung exotic locations was as a schoolboy reciting the lines from 'Valparaiso', written by Oliver St John Gogarty and translated by Padraig de Brun, uncle of the scholar and poet Maire Mac an TSaoi: '*Thainig long o Valparaiso, scaoileadh tead a seol sa chuan.*'

Before we head across the oceans to Valparaiso in Chile and hear about Edward Bransfield and Bernardo O Higgins, the lines below from Irish philosopher Richard Kearney, taken from the wonderful *The Old Ways* by Robert McFarlane, seem very appropriate:

In antiquity, Irish scholars were known ... for their practice of 'navigatio' ... a journey undertaken by boat ... a circular itinerary of exodus and return....The aim was to undergo an apprenticeship to signs of strangeness with a view to becoming more attentive to the meanings of one's own time and place – geographical, spiritual, intellectual.

Paths of long usage exist on water as well as on land. The oceans are seamed with seaways – routes whose course is determined by prevailing winds and currents – rivers are amongst the oldest ways of all. During the winter months, the only route in and out of the remote valley of Zanskar in the Indian Himalayas is along the ice-path formed by a frozen river.

A few weeks ago for *Seascapes* I was a guest of the Irish Naval Service at the Irish Naval Base at Haulbowline, where I was interviewing Commodore Mark Mellett, then Flag Officer Commanding Naval Service, for a future edition of the programme. At the top of Haulbowline Island you can survey the entire entrance to this magnificent deep water harbour, where at one point in our maritime history the *Bounty* tied up and British naval parties raided the south coast to press gang young men into service. Churchill was reluctant to return the ports to this country and through that after the outbreak of war we had Irish Shipping – *sin* however is some *sceal eile....*

Valparaiso is at the heart of making the connection with our seafaring heroes – the first of these is Edward Bransfield from Ballinacurra near Midleton in East Cork. Bransfield is just one of our great maritime explorers.

In 2003 I was fortunate to be in Newfoundland to coincide with the visit of *The Jeanie Johnston* to the North American continent. While in St Johns with Tom MacSweeney we talked with an elderly man who had traversed the waters of the St Lawrence River and had indeed charted some of its water, bringing alive the whole world of exploration and discovery. He told me of setting a course for Lisbon from the Narrows of St Johns and then to the West Indies before returning to Newfoundland with sugar and spices, guided by sextant and the stars.

Marcus Connaughton

Today over 98 per cent of trade into this country still gets here by ship. Think back to the nineteenth century and one of the smartest of Jardine Matheson's schooner-rigged opium clippers, the former tea and fruit carrier *Hellas*. In 1838 she arrived in Canton 124 days out from London, an impressive time for the 92-foot long, 209-ton brigantine.

Hellas was built in 1832 at Whites shipyard in Ferrybank, on the north bank of the River Suir at Waterford, for Charles Bewley of Dublin. A heavily sparred vessel, she spread a large amount of canvas and was worked by a crew of 50.

For six years she traded with China before being acquired for the opium trade in Canton in 1838. *Hellas* was the first ship to carry a cargo of tea directly to Ireland from China. She arrived on 1 March 1835 at Kingstown, now Dun Laoghaire, under the command of Captain A.A. Scanlon with 2,099 chests for Bewleys of Dublin. The East India Company's monopoly of the China tea trade had expired the previous year. In 1855 *Hellas* was lost without trace after leaving Leghorn in Italy.

These clippers were the Formula One vessels of the world's oceans in their day. A clipper ship's sails could generate as much as 3,000 horsepower in a fresh breeze. Square sails were normally set and trimmed from deck, but sailors had to go aloft to work on the yards, standing on footropes (horses) to loose, reef and furl sail and when rigging out or taking in studdingsail booms. A bewildering arrangement of over 200 ropes were attached to the sails and rigging, many of them coming down to the deck. As well as the stays and shrouds that supported the masts there were hoists, downhauls, outhauls, clew lines, leech lines, buntlines, gaskets, sheets, vangs, footropes, strops, ratlines and braces.

Many of these clippers were to be used in the great Californian Gold Rush sailing round the Horn, some never making it as far as Valparaiso on the journey.

What was it that drove Admiral William Brown of Foxford, founder of the Argentine navy; Francis Leopold McClintock of Dundalk; Tom Crean of Annascaul; Ernest Shackleton of Kildare; the inventor of the submarine John Philip Holland of Liscannor; John Barry of Wexford; Francis Crozier of Banbridge; Robert Forde of Kilmurry; Patsy Keohane of Barry's Point; the remarkable Mortimer and Tim McCarthy from Kinsale? With the exception of Holland they all served in the British Navy. These men who explored the southern oceans were following in the routes first navigated by Vasco da Gama and Ferdinand Magellan centuries earlier.

Edward Bransfield was press ganged into the navy from the Dockside in Youghal in 1803 at the age of eighteen. A hardened seafarer, he had fished out of Cobh and Whitegate with his father, the same dockside that was to feature in the film of *Moby Dick* in the 1950s starring Gregory Peck. There are no photographs of Bransfield, however one port that he was very familiar with was Valparaiso in

Chile. The Bransfield Strait, which separates Antarctica from the South Shetland Islands, was discovered by Bransfield in 1820.

Bransfield had built up a considerable reputation as a reliable seafarer and aboard the *Williams* he sailed from Valparaiso on 20 December 1819. The voyage involved sailing more than 2,000 miles from Valparaiso to the South Shetlands, including a 500 mile crossing of the difficult Drake Passage which separates South America from Antarctica. The vessel was a timber two-masted brigantine of 216 tons with no special strengthening to combat the ice.

It took Bransfield nine days to get six miles from Valparaiso but by the 16th of January he reached Livingstone Island. Bransfield's log at the end of this voyage disappeared following his return on 14 April 1820, and were it not for the discovery of the private journal of his midshipman Charles Poynter in the 1990s his part in these discoveries would have gone unheralded.

Two decades after Bransfield had shown the way Francis Crozier mapped large chunks of the seas and land mass. Crozier hailed from Banbridge in County Down and went to sea at thirteen. He travelled on six voyages of discovery to the polar regions and was engaged in the nineteenth century's three great endeavours: navigating the North West Passage, reaching the North Pole and mapping the Antarctic continent.

Robert Forde was born in Kilmurry near Bandon in 1875. Forde was the man who built the wooden hut on McMurdo Sound in January 1911, once occupied by Captain Scott. Forde was a skilled carpenter and deft painter and the hut is still standing – he's pictured alongside Tom Crean.

Patrick or Patsy Keohane joined the British Navy in 1895 at the age of sixteen. Patsy's father was the coxswain of the Courtmacsherry Lifeboat which in 1915 was the first vessel to reach the *Lusitania* torpedoed off the Old Head of Kinsale. Patsy Keohane accompanied Captain Scott in 1911 alongside Tom Crean and Robert Forde.

Our next maritime hero is a native of Clare from Liscannor. His father was the coastguard in nearby Freagh Point near Tra Ban. He went on to become a Christian Brother, taught at the North Monastery in Limerick and Cork and is the inventor of the submarine – his name is John Philip Holland.

Holland is known to all submariners whether in the United States or the Japanese navy for whom he developed prototypes of the earliest vessels. He performed his tests on models in an ornamental pond in the grounds of the North Mon in Cork. He is recognised with a museum in Patterson City, New Jersey, and it's thanks to Clare man Tony Duggan that *Seascapes* has had Holland on our radar for the past few years. In more recent times the National Maritime College of Ireland dedicated their library in honour of Holland and the *ROV Holland 1* is named in his honour.

The *Holland* was small, only 53' long and 9' broad amidships. She was powered by a 2-cylinder 120 h.p. Otto gas engine, built in Germany in 1890, which drove her single screw at a top speed of 9 knots on the surface. She had no bow planes, no periscope, no deck guns, and only a single compartment which did not provide living or messing facilities for the crew.

Each summer the *Holland* would return to Newport for exercises with the Great White Fleet. On one occasion, President Theodore Roosevelt, then on holiday at his summer home on Long Island, ordered her to pick him up at Oyster Bay. The *Holland* took him out for a practice dive, the only time a President of the United States has ever submerged in a submarine.

President Roosevelt noted that the *Holland* crew looked particularly ragged, their dungarees literally rotting away. The captain explained this as a normal result of the heavy fumes that pervaded the tiny ship – acid fumes that would ruin a pair of dungarees in short order. When told that the crew received no extra pay for their rugged duty, President Roosevelt said he'd 'take care of it', and within a few weeks a bill was passed by Congress granting them a $5 pay increase per month!

Commemorative coin in honour of John Philip Holland
(courtesy Central Bank of Ireland)

Crew members aboard this unique craft were subjected to whatever hydrostatic pressure the craft was running under while submerged. To govern this pressure, a free valve abaft the conning tower remained open constantly to allow the air to escape into the sea. The crew could look through the valve into the water above, a fact that never failed to produce a sensation among the passengers brought aboard for instruction.

The craft was so delicately balanced that the weight of a group of midshipmen students had to be determined beforehand, so that an equal weight in lead ballast could be removed before they embarked.

Compared with the large, fast, fleet-type snorkel-equipped submarines of today's Navy, the *Holland* must be considered almost primitive. She carried four air flasks, which supplied the necessary oxygen. Her single hatch was scarcely large enough for a man to squeeze through. In fact, one congressman who visited the submarine at Annapolis was unable to get down the hatch to inspect the boat's interior. The tiny conning tower, equipped with three-inch slits through which the captain could see while running with decks awash, extended almost knee-high from the deck. Smoking below deck was forbidden because of the heavy gasoline and acid fumes.

The *Holland* was the Navy's first serious experiment with a submersible, and the world's first motor-driven submarine. Her crew were the guinea pigs for the experiment. They proved that men could live under the trying conditions existing in such a craft; that a torpedo could be fired accurately under water, while the submarine remained almost invisible; and that the submarine had a great potential as either an offensive or defensive weapon.

At the time she was built by the Electric Boat Company at Bayonne, New Jersey naval strategy viewed the submarine principally as a defensive element, and it was planned to station submarines at all major seaports on the Atlantic and Gulf Coasts for coast defense. Her true offensive potentialities were not realised until the Germans began their submarine operations in World War I.

The *Holland* is no more, but her successors are today among the most effective naval weapons. The men of the 'Silent Service' carry on the proud traditions of courage and devotion to duty established by the volunteers who manned the *USS Holland*, the United States first submarine.

Those following that tradition are harbour masters, islanders, sea captains, lifeboat crews, coastguard and civil defence volunteers, former lighthouse keepers, round the world yachtsmen like Damian Foxall from Derrynane, and Justin Slattery and David Kenefick, our naval and customs service, young men and women in the NMCI, our fishermen and women, and divers and sub-aqua crews around our coast and on our inland waterways.

I was fortunate to be in this magnificent boardroom a few weeks ago for the launch by An Post of a series of Port of Cork stamps reflecting the range of activities that take place on these waters, and indeed *Seascapes* featured a competition for copies of the First Day covers by identifying the designer Steve Simpson. I was reminded of the scene that existed centuries ago with many tall ships tied up along all the quaysides before the age of steam and the *Sirius*.

The *Sirius* was the first ship to cross the Atlantic entirely under steam. Built originally for service in the Irish Sea, the 703-ton vessel, a side-wheeler, was chartered by the British & American Steam Navigation Company and sailed from London to New York by way of Cork in 1838 with 40 passengers. Its 175th anniversary was in March of this year.

Her fuel ran out just short of her destination, but Captain Roberts was determined to complete the passage under steam. He refused to hoist the ship's sails and, instead, fed timbers into the furnace. Sandy Hook, New Jersey, was sighted in time to avert a potential mutiny, and the *Sirius* beat the much larger *Great Western* to New York by a few hours.

In addition to establishing a crossing record, the *Sirius* introduced an important technical innovation, a condenser to recover the fresh water used in the boiler. The vessel was captained by another giant of Irish maritime heritage, Captain Richard Roberts RN of Ardmore, Passage West. The event is commemorated by a beautiful garden just beyond Passage West near the Ferry crossing.

Much like our built heritage, what our maritime heritage needs most of all are advocates – people like the late John de Courcy Ireland, distinguished journalist and sailor Tim Magennis, world class sailor Damian Foxall, Commodore Mark Mellett, Dr Valerie Cummins of IMERC, the RNLI and the Coastguard, Meitheal Mara here in the heart of this city. Get involved – if you have a view let it be known, but most of all if you care, encourage others to do so too.

From The Log of the Molly B, by Pete Hogan

18

Two Hundred Years of
Boat Building in Kinsale

John R. Thuillier

Extract from Traditional Boats of Ireland: History, Folklore and Construction, edited by Crístóir Mac Cárthaigh

In 1805, the Admiralty Dockyard was moved from Kinsale to Haulbowline in Cork harbour where the growing size and sophistication of naval ships could be more easily accommodated. With its closure, the emphasis changed from ship- to boat-building, the focus being now the requirements of the fishing industry and coastal trading, but also pleasure boats. Names associated with boat building in the town at the time include the Barrett and Brown families, and in the latter part of the nineteenth century the firm of Thuillier Brothers. The author of this article is indebted to his grandfather, John Henry Thuillier (RIP 1958), the last member of the Thuillier family to build boats in Kinsale, and an important source of information about boat building in the town. Drawing on his own work diaries and business correspondence, and those of earlier generations, John Henry assembled a detailed record of the family business. His grandfather, Jeremiah Coveney, who was born in 1800, was also an important source of information to him, and before his death he compiled a short biography of his father, Joseph (RIP 1921). These sources, spanning three generations, provide invaluable data on boat building in Kinsale for close on 200 years.

Barrett's Yard was located at what is now the Shearwater Apartments complex, and Cornelius Barrett was the Master Shipwright to whom Joseph Thuillier, John Henry's father, was apprenticed. This was the Cornelius Barrett who, in 1849, produced the drawings of the Kinsale hooker ordered by the House of Commons for its 'Washington' report on fishing boats. The young Thuillier's indenture, dated 1859, set out a seven-year apprenticeship, during which he was bound to not waste the goods of his master or 'commit fornication nor contract matrimony within the said term ... not play cards, dice tables or other unlawful games' and 'not use taverns, ale or play houses'. For the first two and a half years of his apprenticeship, he earned a wage of four shillings per week. In his later life, he recalled his days as a young apprentice:

Kinsale Harbour, c. 1900

At that time, Mr Robert Heard (a prominent landed gentleman) was laying down the lines of the Schooner yacht Echo built by Cornelius Barrett of this town (to whom I served my apprenticeship as a shipwright), a first-rate man. I was then a boy holding the battens and chalk line and it was there I got my first lessons in ship draughting.

There was a keen rivalry between the Brown and Barrett yards. Each had a four-oared gig, manned by apprentices, which raced to an incoming ship (which was signalled from Castlepark), the first gig to reach the vessel claiming the repairs for the ship while it was in port. There was similar competition between fishbuyers who raced out to the harbour-bound fleet in the morning to contract a price before the auction ashore. Such competition contributed to the phenomenon of yawl rowing, still popular on the Cork coast.

Joseph married Anne, daughter of Jeremiah Coveney, a well-regarded Kinsale boat builder and, with his brothers, Michael and Henry, opened a yard at World's End. From here they expanded into related maritime interests such as ship-owning, fishing and yachting. Joseph was a dynamic individual and for 50 years was a member of Kinsale Harbour Board, holding the position of chairman for 30 of these. It was during this time that sixteen tidal piers were filled in on the water front and the Pier Head and Road to cater for the increase in traffic, particularly fishing. He became active in the Fenian movement and, following the 1867 Rising, was tipped off that he and other activists were about to be arrested. Without delay, he joined a westbound vessel off the Old Head of Kinsale, bound for America. During his exile, he was kept informed by his mother Ellen with news of the family and business, her letters warning that it was 'not safe to return home yet'. Her warnings were based on information from a family acquaintance with contacts in Dublin Castle.

When he eventually returned to Kinsale in 1868, Joseph continued to develop the business, but it would appear that conflict with authority and local Admiralty personnel persisted for a time. An

Tertia, built by Thuilliers

incident on the death of his mother in March 1874 illustrates the point. Three crew members of a Navy gunboat pulled down the ensign which was flown at half-mast on the *Ellen Thuillier*, one of the family's fishing boats. Thuillier demanded and eventually received an apology from the captain of the gunboat. Much later, in 1921, the year he died, the old Fenian spark was alive when he declared.

'This fishing provides a blessing as it gives good employment to those who wanted it most, but the English capitalist has his eye on it and soon will have it altogether. He waited while it was getting developed and then tried his hand with steam trawlers and with abundant capital, fitted them with the best machinery to be had and let them loose on the fishing grounds which they very soon exhausted.' ... Not content with that, they built a class of steam drifter, which fish off our Irish coast and take the fish direct to the English buyer, cutting the people of this country completely off.

There is a laconic mention in Thuillier's work diary, for Tuesday 25 January 1887, of the launch of a new boat for what was then known as the Royal Life Boat Institution. He tells us, 'She hung on the ways for half an hour – we got the screw to her and she went off beautifully. Got three ton of metal from Perrots and got it in her. Got card from Institution.' While the diary entry appears prosaic, the launch of a lifeboat was a significant event for the town. On the day of the launch, the daily work routine for the 25 to 30 people employed in various capacities in the yard continued regardless. Lengthy sea trials were conducted by a Mr Brady and Lieutenant Tipping, Inspector of Life Boats, on 21 March 1887, and both men were satisfied with the 'unquestionable safety of the vessel in the event of a collision at sea as she is divided into three watertight compartments.'

The family interests in the sea included shipping. One of their larger vessels was the schooner Emilie, which ran aground in the Mersey on a voyage from Garston, bound for Crosshaven with a cargo of coal. She was described as well found with a crew of four men and two passengers. Having struck on a bank, she sank and became a danger to shipping. The authorities put a charge aboard and destroyed the vessel. All hands were saved.

The Thuilliers enjoyed sailing for pleasure and built some very fine yachts. Of the Irish-based yachts listed in Lloyd's Register of Yachts (1925), the only Irish-built boat was the a wooden cutter produced by Thuillier Brothers in 1898. Tertia was 35-foot LOA (length overall), 28-foot LWL (length water-line), 8-foot 6-inch beam and 4-foot 9-inch draught; sails were Ratsey and Lapthorn, with sail area of 1,005 square feet. She is still fondly remembered by the older generation in Kinsale, where a mythology surrounds her 'David and Goliath' struggles with the larger Donegan's *Gull*. The whole town would turn out at the Fort Hill or Compass Hill to watch the end of the annual 'Ocean Race' from Cork.

Individual members of the Thuillier family had their own boats – *Glance, Heroine, Spray, Swallow* and *Truent*. In the diaries, there are repeated references to racing in Kinsale. A beautiful trophy, presented by the Munster Fusiliers stationed at Charles Fort, was won by Michael Thuillier in 1873, and is still raced for at Kinsale Yacht Club.

From *Traditional Boats of Ireland – History, Folklore and Construction* edited by Crístóir Mac Cárthaigh, published by The Collins Press, www.collinspress.ie.

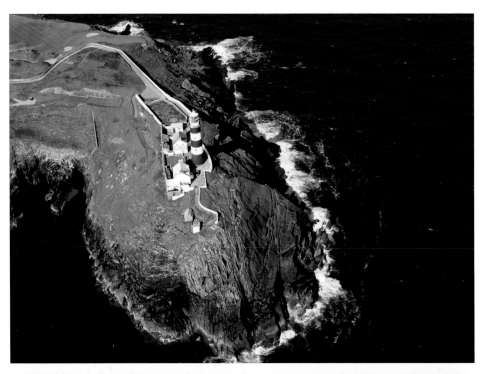

Two views of the Old Head of Kinsale (photos by Dennis Horgan)

19

The Sinking of the Lusitania

Patrick O'Sullivan

An extract from The Sinking of the Lusitania – Unravelling the Mysteries by Patrick O'Sullivan

Queenstown became the town of the dead as the temporary morgues filled with bodies. The anguish, and sometimes anger, of the townspeople was aggravated at the sight of helpless, half-clad, soaked and shivering women struggling over the piers at Queenstown as they disembarked from the rescue boats. Some unfortunates held precious babes in arms, while others moaned for some lost soul. Dishevelled, white-faced men, some without clothing, formed part of this grim procession of humanity descending on Queenstown. The poignant grief was deepened by the sight of rows of bodies of babies and children as they lay, calm-faced like dolls, in the makeshift houses of death. Each newly arrived boat brought more dead to swell the ever-increasing numbers in the morgues. The tug *Polzee* arrived with sixteen dead, including three babies; the corpses were brought ashore on stretchers, while the sailors carried the three babies in their arms. The dispatches stated that the babies had retained a freshness and suppleness of life as if death had not been painful. As they came ashore, the officers on the pier saluted, civilians lifted their hats and women wept. One of the dead was little Betty Bretherton, who was turned over to her heartbroken mother who had miraculously survived the disaster.

The town opened its heart to the legions of devastated survivors who made their way ashore; hotels and private homes opened their doors to the bewildered victims. Surgeons, doctors and over a hundred nurses volunteered their services to aid the injured. Drapers, as well as private citizens, gave clothes and blankets. Stunned, and in many cases hysterical, the survivors thankfully accepted the hospitality of the townspeople. Many had been in the water for hours and nearly all had discarded as much clothing as possible to keep themselves afloat. Women came ashore wrapped in blankets, several wore men's clothing, nearly all were shoeless, and a great many were without socks. The locals and the authorities made every possible effort to alleviate their suffering. Many, having reached the safety of Queenstown, later died of exposure or their terrible injuries; morbid crowds surrounded the temporary morgues, where bodies awaited identification.

From the gloom and horror came stories of the unselfish heroism of those who went to martyrs' graves and sacrificed their lives for others. Some escaped death by a hair's breadth as they struggled to save lives. Alfred Vanderbilt, the multimillionaire sportsman, and his valet, showed great heroism as they tirelessly assisted women and children to the lifeboats. Though Vanderbilt could not swim, he gallantly took off his lifejacket and placed it around the body of a young woman. As he went to seek another lifejacket, the ship took its death plunge and he perished in a vortex of swirling water and hissing steam. Charles Frohman, the impresario, also showed remarkable courage when he handed his lifejacket to a lady in distress. He also perished with the ship and his floating body was later recovered from the sea to join the ranks of the dead.

A pretty nineteen-year-old Irish immigrant named Annie Kelly, from Galway, suffered a cruel irony when she made a round trip

Coffins in the mass grave

on the ill-fated *Lusitania*. Annie's boyfriend, William Murphy, had emigrated earlier to America and Annie hoped to join and marry him soon after her arrival. As an immigrant, she was obliged to undergo a medical examination before entering America. The examination revealed a heart defect which excluded Annie from entry because it would limit her ability to earn a living. She was then interned at Ellis Island for deportation as immigration law decreed. In such instances, the ship that brought the immigrant to America was obliged to return that person at its own expense. This meant travelling in steerage for the return trip. When Annie's brother learned of her plight and confinement on Ellis Island, he took energetic steps to seek an exemption. He journeyed to Boston to petition the Mayor on the basis that he would personally assume all responsibility and care for Annie in the event of her health preventing her from working. He encountered one frustrating delay after another, but was eventually granted an exemption. He immediately left with all haste for New

York only to discover that the *Lusitania* had departed just half an hour earlier. Annie perished in the disaster and her body was never found.

Elbert Hubbard, the author, publisher and lecturer, also went down with the ship. He was journeying to Europe to become a war correspondent. He had joked to friends, 'I may meet a mine or submarine over there, or I may hold friendly converse with a bullet in the trenches.' During his last voyage, standing on the *Lusitania's* deck, he made a prophetic statement to a reporter: 'Speaking from a strictly personal point of view, I would not mind if they did sink the ship. It might be a good thing for me. I would drown with her, and that's about the only way I could succeed in my ambition to get into the Hall of Fame. I'd be a regular hero and go right to the bottom.' Elbert Hubbard had already condemned the German Kaiser with his vitriolic pen for his policy of militarism which saw the devastation of Belgium. He issued a scathing indictment against him in his magazine, the *Philistine*. The article was titled 'Who lifted the lid off Hell?' and had the following to say, 'Bill Kaiser has a withered hand and a running ear, also he has a shrunken soul, and a mind that reeks of egomania. He is swollen like a drowned pup, with a pride that stinks. He never wrote a letter nor a message wherein he did not speak of God as if the Creator was waiting for him in the lobby. God is with us, God is destroying our enemies, God is giving us victories and I am accountable only to my conscience and God.' Ironically it was Germany's policy of militarism that destined Hubbard and his writer wife to death on the last voyage of the *Lusitania*.

The entire Crompton family of father, mother and six children, ranging from six months to thirteen years, were lost on the Lusitania. Paul Crompton spent a considerable part of his life in the Orient, where he learned the Chinese language. The extent of his travels is illustrated by the birthplaces of his children. Stephen the eldest son, whose body was recovered, was born in Vladivostok in Eastern Russia. Catherine, aged twelve, was born in London, thirteen-year-old

Alberta was born in South America and the other children, Romley aged nine, John aged five and baby Peter aged six months, were born in Philadelphia.

After a successful season of engagements in America, Hamish Mackay, the Scottish baritone and musician, was due to return to his wife and son in Edinburgh. He had performed at Carnegie Hall, New York, on 24 June 1914, at the celebration of the battle of Bannockburn. He had a great love of his native Scottish music, which he promoted at every opportunity. Hamish, who was exhausted and run down from his hectic tour, eagerly anticipated home and much-needed rest as he planned his return on the *Lusitania*. His wife, however, had a sense of foreboding about the ship and wrote to warn him to be sure to sail on the American liner *New York City* as the Germans would never dare torpedo a neutral passenger ship. She further warned him to take out American papers as soon as possible, so that Germans who might board his ship could not take him prisoner. However, the Monday after the *Lusitania* departed from New York, Mrs Mackay received a letter from her husband advising her that he intended to sail on the *Lusitania* and looked forward to meeting her in a few days. She was very apprehensive at receiving this news and spent the next few days in anxious anticipation of his safe arrival. Her worst fears were confirmed on the Friday evening, when she heard of the tragedy. A family friend, one Mr Angus, journeyed to Queenstown in a futile search for her husband. Having examined the morgues in vain, he interviewed many of the survivors, who recalled that his lost colleague had sung beautifully on Thursday evening at the ship's concert and promised to sing again on Friday. After his week long stay, Angus came to accept the worst and abandoned all hope of finding his friend alive.

In total, 1,198 lives were lost on the *Lusitania*. Behind each one there is a sad story to be told. One cannot imagine the last thoughts of the doomed and the dying. Only God can have known their agony of mind, their tortures of despair, their last fleeting memories of home and safety, their regrets for having ignored the last-minute warnings of the German Embassy, their concern for distant children or parents, the hopelessness in the realisation that the war visited them with an unjust death sentence. Of the drowned, 127 were Americans, 79 were children including 39 infants under the age of two years. Of the 1,198 lost victims, approximately 200 corpses were recovered from the sea. The remainder were never found. In August of the same year, a badly decomposed and bloated male corpse was washed up on the coast near Galway. From items of clothing on the body, it was identified as American and prepared for shipping to the United States on the Allan liner *Hesperian*, which was ironically torpedoed by Schwieger in command of U-20. This tragic coincidence earned the macabre distinction of an American citizen being committed to the deep on two occasions by the same assailant.

Funeral cortege

Worldwide, anxious and distraught people poured into Cunard's offices seeking information about passengers and crew. Personal enquiries were supplemented by a steady shower of telegrams from all parts. The jingle of telephone bells played an accompaniment to the frantic efforts of overworked employees engaged in revising lists and answering questions. Clerks were obliged to double check their information before releasing it. First releases of messages were made at Cunard's head office in Liverpool. Most of the men and women who made enquiries for relatives or friends manifested their grief; some fainted, others became hysterical, tears streaming down their faces. Those who received good news sobbed with relief as they heard the name of a loved one read off the list of those saved. Some shouted names to clerks only to receive the ominous reply, 'not yet received'; this caused them to beg that the lists be re-checked or to ask if by chance it was a spelling error, as the name 'must be there'. Crowds lingered all day around Cunard offices in anticipation of revised lists which might end their nightmare.

On Monday, 10 May, three days after the sinking of the ship, the awful crime was marked by the passage of a funeral cortege through the streets of Queenstown. Reverently and mournfully the town paid full honours of the nation to the bodies of 140 men, women and children who lost their lives on the *Lusitania*. When the funeral started, people sensed the full horror of the tragedy as the long line of coffins slowly disappeared over the hill behind the town on their way to the graveyard. The bustle in the temporary morgues was replaced by an eerie silence as the dead made their final journey.

From *The Sinking of the Lusitania – Unravelling the Mysteries* by Patrick O'Sullivan, published by The Collins Press, www.collinspress.ie

Top – Water Wags off Dun Laoghaire (photo by David Branigan/Oceansports)
Bottom – Asgard on display at the National Museum of Ireland, Collins Barracks,
Dublin (photo by Marcus Connaughton)

20

Ireland's Sailing Tradition

W.M. Nixon

William M. Nixon has been writing about sailing in Ireland and internationally for many years, with his work appearing in leading sailing publications on both sides of the Atlantic. A member for ten years of the Council of the Irish Yachting Association (now the Irish Sailing Association), he has been writing for, and at times editing, Ireland's national sailing magazine since its earliest version more than forty years ago. He currently writes the weekly blog 'Sailing on Saturday' on Afloat.ie. This piece was broadcast on Seascapes on RTÉ Radio 1 as a Thomas Davis Lecture in 2002.

It's definitely a minority interest, this enthusiasm for boats and sailing. It's a peculiar quirk of character. Down the ages, majority opinion – the popular view – has been agin it.

So why do we who enjoy boats find it so pleasant being afloat and how can we explain it to other people? Should we bother?

For instance, the Bible, the New Testament and the Book of Revelations of St John the Divine, tells of his vision of the ultimate heaven. In Chapter 21, Verse 1:

'And I saw a new heaven and a new earth: for the first heaven and the first earth were passed away; and there was no more sea'.

Quite! Fast forward now to eighteenth century London, a thriving metropolis whose wealth is based largely on maritime trade. Despite that, Dr Samuel Johnson, the opinion former of his own and subsequent ages, is in no doubt about the unpleasant reality of the world afloat:

'Sir, when a man gets to like sea life, he is not fit to live on land....'

Another time, Johnson went into more detail:

'Sir, no man will be a sailor who has contrivance enough to get himself into a jail; for being in a ship is being in jail, with the chance of being drowned.... A man in jail has more room, better food, and commonly better company....'

It could of course be argued that the type of sailing being discussed by these two worthies is a seafaring borne of harsh economic necessity. But surely that makes any tendency to go afloat for pleasure even more perverse. After all, both St John the Divine and Sam Johnson are telling us that ships and the sea are simply hellish. So what on earth would they make of those of us who like boats and sailing for their own sakes?

Such a one was Ireland's St Columba of Derry and Iona who exuberantly declared in AD 563 (in June, one would hazard, during a week of unusually good weather):

'What joy to sail the crested sea, and watch the waves beat white upon the Irish shore'

Even if the nineteenth century translation by James Clarence Mangan is a bit over the top, there's no doubting the genuine enthusiasm which inspired Columba. Nevertheless, he'd be a brave man who would declaim the joys of sailing the crested sea to a crowd of seasick passengers on the Cork-Swansea ferry in a November gale. This delight in boats, undoubtedly a minority thing, is very genuine.

Maybe it's got something to do with genetics. At some stages in human development, particularly in certain environments, a peculiar personal enthusiasm for going afloat, and going places in boats, must have been a very useful survival mechanism.

Mankind's recreations today are a throwback to former vitally necessary skills and interests which evolved from quirks of character. The special abilities of upland shepherds of old gave us today's mountaineering. We are told that angling is one of the modern world's most popular pastimes, yet, in times past, an enthusiasm for fishing could mean the difference between life and death. Think of today's amateur enthusiasms for hunting, gardening, athletic sports, team events, animal breeding and heaven only knows what else, and we see specific modern interests – not necessarily shared by everyone – which hark back to a time when such interests resulted in survival.

The point is, though, that early man happened to discover an enthusiasm for special interests which incidentally worked to his advantage in the survival stakes. Today, each of those interests survives in the contemporary world's bewildering array of sports, hobbies and pastimes and in each modern individual, different genetic patterns lead to a different pattern of pursuits and passions.

This in turn can lead to total incomprehension of someone else's special interest patterns, such that today, although there are people who have a broad general interest in all sports, equally there are many who are so passionately involved as participants in one particular sport that they cannot see they cannot see the attractions of any other activity. It's a case of one man's sport being another man's poison.

It could of course be argued that Ireland, of all places, is ideally suited for the development of boat sports, and particularly sailing sports. After all, not only are we an island, but the entire territory is criss-crossed by fine rivers and extensive lakes, over which there is usually an ample supply of wind.

Strategically located as an island to the west of Europe, Ireland at first glance appears to have all the geographical requirements to be a premier maritime nation. However the fulfilment of geographical factors is only part – and arguably only a small part – of the requirements for national maritime greatness. There are very few single island maritime nations. Japan, for instance, is undoubtedly a maritime nation, but it has many islands. It's an archipelago and the history of maritime achievement suggests that coastal people, rather than island dwellers, tend to become maritime nations.

Think, for instance, of the Phoenicians, those heroic early voyagers. They weren't islanders at all. Their home territory was a crowded strip of coastline in the eastern Mediterranean, with the presence of powerful neighbours in the hinterland stimulating a tendency to look seaward for means of commercial expansion and self-expression.

Nearer our own time, the Vikings may in some cases have become islanders, but they started out as coastal dwellers in an increasingly crowded land mass. Think, too, of the great Portuguese and Dutch voyagers, and the strongly maritime nations they represented. In both cases, they were coastal dwellers, with irritatingly powerful neighbours firmly established inland.

As for the great English voyagers of the Elizabethan era, they might have liked to think of themselves as the hardy maritime representatives of a true island nation. But, the reality is that England is not an island – it is barely half of the total area of the island of Britain. Yet it is the dominant but inaccurate picture which the English have of themselves as an island nation which has led to a general expectation that successful island nations will inevitably be powerful maritime nations.

England's sense of island-ness was more to do with its pride in being cut off from continental Europe, rather than island reality. Even within the relatively small English land mass, we find that the most active mariners tended to come from somewhat impoverished coastal areas, such as South Devon, where the best hope of personal advancement was to be found in going to sea.

By ancient European standards of settlement and population, Ireland is the new boy on the block. The first visitors were undoubtedly intrepid voyagers but the first settlers were seafarers only from the necessity of having to cross the North Channel from Scotland.

They were probably mighty glad to get off the sea, and they came ashore to find a fertile land flowing in milk and honey. As long as the population remained below a certain level, the living was relatively easy, and the sea tended to be seen as a useful defence, rather than the high road to adventure and wealth. Yet even in those relatively contented times, there were those who manifested an almost unnatural enthusiasm for going afloat in small boats.

The story of Ireland's seafaring monks is so entwined with myth and propaganda that some plucky individuals have actually dared to suggest that St Brendan the Navigator never really existed! But the voyaging of St Brendan is as important to Irish seafaring as the plays of Shakespeare are to English literature.

We know some folk doubt that Shakespeare even wrote the plays. To which a reasonable reply is that if he didn't write them, then they were written by someone of the same name. So for those who would argue that the great Irish voyager was not St Brendan, all we can say is: maybe so, but there undoubtedly were some remarkable seafaring achievements made by someone of the same name.

That there was great Irish voyaging at this time is attested to by the Vikings. As they spread out across the Atlantic, they reported finding communities of Irish monks on many remote islands. Technologically speaking, the Vikings were much more advanced seafarers than the Irish. So, how had those early monks managed to undertake great voyages in considerably primitive craft?

The final answer, surely, is that they simply enjoyed sailing the sea. Certainly they may have given all sorts of spiritual and religious reasons for setting out into the unknown. But unless they actually

enjoyed it, unless they became – in a sense – sea creatures themselves, there was just no way they were going to survive and willingly endure discomfort which is beyond our imagination today.

I'm not suggesting that you need an austerely monastic frame of
mind in order to go to sea for pleasure, but it helps. However, not all
pleasure afloat involves epic voyaging. In fact, most of it is on a very
modest scale indeed.

Ireland is an extremely watery place, and virtually all of it is close
to navigable waters. So although in ancient times the horse may have
been the preferred means of transport for those who could afford it,
the attraction and relative convenience of boats was not overlooked.
Where boats were used for personal transport, they soon became a
source of pride and relaxation. It's an intriguing snippet of history
to learn that, as long ago as the twelfth century, the Maguires of Fermanagh enjoyed the use of their own pleasure craft on Lough Erne.

One of Ireland's leading offshore sailors, Gordon Maguire, is a
direct descendant of those water sporting Maguires of Fermanagh
– his grandfather left Enniskillen as a sixteen year old to seek his
fortune in Dublin. Not all of today's boat enthusiasts can claim a
sailing bloodline which goes back at least nine centuries. But, as it
happens, in Gordon's case it is even more thorough than that, for
on his mother's side he is descended from the English Elizabethan
sea warrior Sir John Hawkins, whose family eventually settled in
County Wicklow. Follow that, as they say.

However, it is the Fermanagh connection which is most marked,
and that in turn reminds us that the inland waterways and lakes have
played a hugely important role in the development of recreational
boating in Ireland. And it is the quiet pleasure of exploring the inland waterways which has given a quote – albeit from boating on the
Upper Thames in England – which boat people often resort to when,
usually in some desperation, they try to explain their hobby to non-
enthusiasts. It's from Kenneth Grahame's *The Wind in the Willows*:

'Believe me, my young friend, there is nothing – absolutely nothing – half so much worth doing as simply messing about in boats.'

That this well-worn quotation is used so often to justify the attraction of boats to a non-believer reveals our frustration in trying to explain our enthusiasm. Boat folk may not necessarily be men or women of action, but they like to think they are people of few words who get things done. Thus they'd prefer their interpersonal communications to be monosyllabic, their written information to be precise, and their songs to be simple. They like to think that they get on with sailing the sea without making a song and dance about it.

In fact true sailors' songs – apart from their working songs – are more usually about the joys of the harbour and the waterfront, and the rough pleasures thereof, rather than about sailing the sea. It is only a basically land-bound poet who would ever romance the lonely sea and the sky. And as for a grey dawn breaking, if I never see one again it will be too soon. So as an aside, if you want a song which captures the practical and harsh reality of sailing and seafaring, you get it in the Caribbean with 'Sloop John B'.

Yet boat owning is character-building. It is a highly educational glimpse of old age. Maintaining a boat is largely a matter of making sure that the bits and pieces which should move smoothly continue to do so, while those things which should be firmly secured in one place continue to maintain their position. But as with the aging human body, so with boats it is the case that things which shouldn't bend do, while things which should, don't.

People have been messing about in boats in Ireland for the sheer fun of it for much longer than is generally realised. The tendency to mess about in boats affects all classes and all intellects. It has been said that anyone wishing to become a millionaire should first become a billionaire, and then acquire a mega-yacht. And as for intellects, one of the most impressive to settle in Ireland was Sir William Petty, the Surveyor General in the seventeenth century.

Petty personified the old saying that if you want anything done, then ask a busy man to do it. One of his many interests was in the potential of double-hulled sailing boats – catamarans as they're called today. He had one built in Dublin in 1663 and demonstrated its remarkable performance in the mouth of the Liffey, pacing it successfully against a small sailing boat belonging to a Dutch ship which happened to be in Dublin port at the time together with a locally based *'pleasure boatte'*.

This quaint exercise was re-enacted in 1991 by maritime historian Hal Sisk, and once again the *Simon and Jude* – as contemporary Dubliners nicknamed the original catamaran – was the winner. But perhaps the most intriguing aspect of the whole business was the fact that the presence of a locally-based sailing *'pleasure boatte'* in Dublin Bay was mentioned in the original account without comment, suggesting that an early form of yachting was already an accepted part of the scene.

The word 'yacht' comes from the Dutch *jaghten* (to hunt). As early as the fifteenth century, the Dutch did much of the pioneering work in establishing yachting as an identifiable activity, and they went pleasure sailing in hunting boats with manners put on them. The activity spread to other countries, and we know that by the late eighteenth century, when the Grand Canal Dock was formally opened by the Lord Lieutenant in April 1796, he performed the ceremony from the vice regal yacht *Dorset* in the presence of a fleet of pleasure yachts.

The real interest in that mention of a fleet of yachts in Dublin's Liffey in 1796 lies in the fact that it was all happening several decades before we get any historical record of any organised yachting activity on Ireland's east coast.

On the south coast Cork Harbour became for ever inscribed in world sailing history with the establishment of the Water Club of the Harbour of Cork, complete with its own wonderful rules for waterborne and club activity, in 1720. It was the world's first true sailing club. Today, the Royal Cork Yacht Club at Crosshaven is its contemporary incarnation.

Some pernickety yachting historians may claim that the continuous existence of this club is questionable, pointing out that no written records exist of its activities in the latter half of the eighteenth century. But if you go into the National Gallery in Dublin, there's a fine painting by Nathaniel Grogan of Cork Harbour in 1785. Prominent in it is a yacht of the Water Club, in stylish seagoing order a good 65 years after the club's foundation. So the fact that the written records of Water Club activity are sparse need not bother us. Obviously then – as now – there was simply no money to be made from writing about sailing!

The founders of the Cork Water Club cruised about in semi-naval formations. It took a surprisingly long time for yacht racing to develop in any organised way, but needless to say it probably happened in Ireland. In terms of world sailing history, the next two clubs were founded in 1770, one in Devon in England, and the other – still going strong – on Lough Ree in Ireland. It is likely that both organised some sort of racing, but oddly enough the first club specifically set up anywhere for the purpose of racing didn't happen until 1820, when the Lough Erne Yacht Club came into being in County Fermanagh, the most watery of all Ireland's counties.

It's said that for six months of the year the lakes are in Fermanagh, and for the other six months Fermanagh is in the lakes. Be that as it may, isn't this where we came in? The Maguires of Fermanagh had their trail blazing fleet of pleasure craft on Lough Erne in the twlefth century and those same waters witnessed this major sailing development 700 years later.

For the establishment of Lough Erne Yacht Club for the purposes of racing in 1820 was part of the beginning of modern yachting, which started to find its feet with the great peace which began with the end of the Napoleonic Wars in 1815.

Most of the history of this modern yachting since 1815 – in Ireland as elsewhere – is well documented. If people don't know of it, then it's probably because they prefer to live for the present, and get on with their own lives, rather than be as interested in history as historians think they ought to be.

With every passing year, my sympathy is increasingly with the non–historians. If it comes to that, I'm beginning to wonder about the value of the written word. After all, while historians are busy telling us how important history is (and they would, wouldn't they?) isn't it writers who preach on about the importance of literature?

There you go. Anyway, perhaps the real interest of Irish sailing history since 1815 is to be found in relating it to the big picture, whether it be sad or spectacular. For instance, today we find that the West of Ireland is a significant coastline for expansion and energy in sailing. It happened before, in 1832, when the grandly named Royal Western of Ireland Yacht Club was founded at Kilrush on the Shannon Estuary by Maurice O'Connell, the uncle of Daniel O'Connell. It prospered, and by 1838 there were 18 substantial yachts based in Kilrush. Yet by 1850, they had all gone, blown away by the Famine.

It may seem crass even to mention the decline of pleasure sailing in the context of a massive human tragedy like the Famine, but surely it helps us to understand why such a special importance attaches to the contemporary revival of Kilrush as a recreational harbour, and the expanding activities of the 'new' Western Yacht Club there.

Today, offshore racing plays a major role in sailing, and it first emerged as Ireland came back to life after the Famine. The world's first recognisable modern offshore race took place between Dublin Bay and Cork Harbour in July 1860. The winner by just three minutes after a cliff hanger finish was the amateur skipper Henry O Bryan of Cork racing Sir John Arnott's 39-ton cutter *Sybil*. Second was J.W. Cannon's 80-ton *Peri* and third, only two minutes astern on the finish line in Cork Harbour, was the 90-ton schooner *Kingfisher*, owned by Cooper Penrose.

These were big boats, and the uneven nature of Ireland's growing prosperity was reflected in the fact that, in the 1870s and 1880s, the yacht tonnage registered with the Royal St George Yacht Club on

Dublin Bay was amongst the largest in the world. Yet by the 1890s, the figure had significantly declined. In the Irish context, the growth of the Land League surely had something to do with it.

In fact, even within the sailing community, the late nineteenth century saw a reaction against the vulgar extravagance which had characterised the heights of the Victorian era, and it resulted in yet another Irish sailing invention – one design racing – which started on Dublin Bay in 1887. The notion of sailing skill rather than expenditure being the basis of winning was anathema to many, but that's where we are now in Irish club sailing.

The struggle for independence was a difficult business for much of the sailing community, as sailing inevitably had close links with naval power, which in turn was central to Britain's sense of imperial mission. Nevertheless, amateur sailors made their contribution. Erskine Childers' adventures with the *Asgard* are of course well known and considerable. But with every passing year, there is growing awareness of the achievement of Childers' friend Conor O'Brien of Foynes, who between 1923 and 1925 made a significant voyage right round the world south of the great Capes in the little ketch *Saoirse*, built to his own designs in Baltimore, West Cork.

It was O'Brien's way of celebrating the establishment of the Irish Free State. Today, his splendid achievement is central to world sailing history and those of us who sail are in awe of what he did. And we can identify with him, too. For like us, he was misunderstood by those about him. His cousin Denis Gwynn, the writer, reckoned that O'Brien had wasted his life, for he had shown early promise as an architect. In a world in which people seriously think that Conor O'Brien of the *Saoirse* would have been much better staying at his architect's drawing board instead of voyaging around the world, how on earth can we who only mess about in boats hope to be understood, let alone appreciated?